5-Minute
Math Problem
of the Day
for Young Learners

180 Fast & Fun Reproducible Problems & Puzzles that
Help You Build Early Math Skills Every Day of the School Year

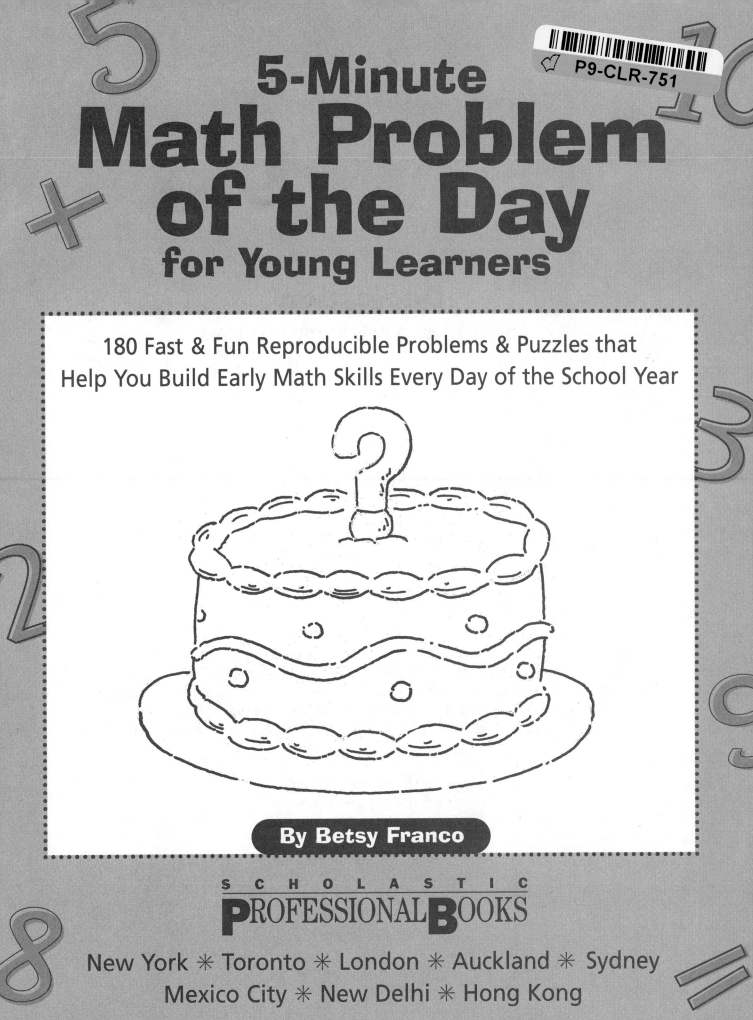

By Betsy Franco

SCHOLASTIC
PROFESSIONAL BOOKS

New York ✳ Toronto ✳ London ✳ Auckland ✳ Sydney
Mexico City ✳ New Delhi ✳ Hong Kong

Dedication
For Rick, who was in my first class.

Developed by Raindrop Publishing LLC
Cover design by George Miyer
Interior design by Debra Spindler
Interior illustration by Susan Calitri
Edited by Lisa Trumbauer

ISBN: 0-439-20151-9
Copyright © 2001 by Betsy Franco
All rights reserved.

12 11 10 9 8 7 6 5 4 3 2 1

Table of Contents

Problem Solving has never looked so good! *5-Minute Math Problem of the Day for Young Learners* is a perfect package for primary children. It's funny, hands-on, fun, seasonal, and age-appropriate.

This treasury of short daily problems is just what you need to introduce the process of problem solving in a relaxed, enjoyable way. Everyone can collaborate as they practice early problem solving skills without pressure.

Book Organization

The story problems presented here are arranged monthly, starting with September. For each month, you have approximately twenty problems. The problems at the beginning of a month tend to be easy, gradually increasing in difficulty as the month progresses. Some problems also include "Extras," which offer a more challenging version of the problem.

The book is designed so you can follow it systematically on a day-to-day basis. Because the problems are related to the months, you can share them with children while tying them to corresponding seasons and holidays. However, do not feel locked in to this monthly arrangement. If children need practice with a particular skill, feel free to select a story problem from another chapter that focuses on that skill.

Skills Index

The upper right corner of each activity has a skills box that calls out the skill being reinforced. In the back of the book, you will find a Skills Index (page 109). If you choose not to follow the book sequence, look up the skill you wish to teach that day. Story problems for that skill are listed, making it easy for you to apply the problems to the needs of your class.

The story problems in this book cover a variety of math concepts that span the whole math curriculum and correlate with the NCTM Standards. As children enjoy and solve the problems, they will build and sharpen such skills as:

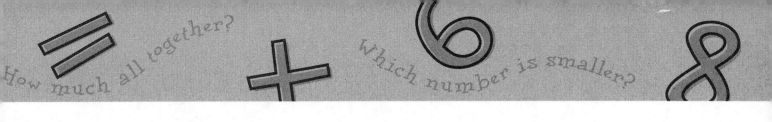
- ✳ sorting and classifying
- ✳ recognizing patterns
- ✳ counting and skip-counting
- ✳ adding and subtracting
- ✳ understanding place value
- ✳ time, money, measurement
- ✳ pre-multiplication
- ✳ estimating and number sense

- ✳ ordering and comparing
- ✳ completing patterns
- ✳ graphing
- ✳ identifying shapes
- ✳ using a calculator
- ✳ fractions
- ✳ pre-division
- ✳ logical reasoning

Language is another important element of the story problems. Most problems are presented as little stories with fun characters that need help finding a solution. Problems are also set up as riddles and rhymes. And most have a story context that will inspire children's imaginations and tickle their brain cells.

Preparation

Before passing out a story problem, read it over to determine how you would like to present it. For example, you may wish to write rhymes on paper for the class to read aloud together. Or, you may wish to set up bar graphs to save time during the lesson. Also, some activities may have patterns that can be reproduced and placed in a pocket chart for easy manipulation. A few activities may require students to work with manipulatives you have on hand.

You might also wish to decide how children should work through the problem. For example, children could solve the problem individually, with a partner, in a group setting or as a whole class. Decide which strategy works best with your class.

Each story problem has been written to speak directly to the student. Reproduce the appropriate amount so each child has a copy. Cut the story problem from the page on the dotted lines to further focus children's attention on each individual problem.

How to Use

Upon passing out the story problem and arranging children in desired groups, read the story problem with them. Make sure children can read and understand the words. Encourage them to ask any questions, then challenge them to work together (or independently) to solve the problem, applying the appropriate math operation.

To structure the lesson, you might set a specific time limit of 5 to 10 minutes. Stress to children that they should have fun with the problems, perhaps pretending they are helping the characters or imagining themselves as part of the story-problem situation.

As children work on the story problems, they are encouraged to consider such questions as:

∗ What does the problem ask?

∗ What information does the problem give?

∗ Which math operation should I use?

∗ Will it help solve the problem to draw a picture?

∗ Will it help solve the problem to make a list or table?

∗ What pattern do I see?

∗ Can I use "guess and check" to solve the problem?

∗ Should I solve the problem with manipulatives?

∗ Should I solve the problem with paper and pencil, with a calculator, or can I solve it in my head?

After the suggested time, invite students to share their answers. Write their ideas on the chalkboard or on chart paper, prompting students to explain how they solved the problem. Since problems may have more than one correct answer, make sure you credit all students with a job well done. An Answer Key is provided (see page 105) at the end of the book to guide your solutions and explanations.

Have Fun!

In *5-Minute Math Problem of the Day for Young Learners* you can guide the children as they measure Jack's Beanstalk, line up penguins in order of size, answer riddles about shapes, and do "squirrel math problems" with Sally Squirrel. Watch as the children cooperate and relax while practicing problem solving together on a daily basis. If you forget the problem of the day, children will be sure to remind you!

September

Which number is larger?

What shapes do you see?

How many do they have?

Name _____

The Name Game

Play the Name Game with a partner. Wear your name tags.

How many letters in your first name? _____   How many in your partner's? _____

Whose name has more letters? _____   Whose name has fewer? _____

That's how you play the name game!

<u>Extra:</u> Compare the number of letters in your last names, too!

Anna

Name _____

Name Sort

Place your name tag with the name tags of your classmates.
Now sort the name tags into "Girls" and "Boys."

How many are in each group?   Girls _____   Boys _____

Can you find other ways to sort the name tags?
Write your ideas on the back. Then try them out.

7

How many in each group?

What patterns do you see?

Name _____

Off to School

Ask your classmates how they get to school. By car? By bike? By bus? Do they walk?
Color in one square for each answer.

car																							
bike																							
bus																							
feet																							

How do most of your classmates get to school? _____

Name _____

One Friend a Day

Tommy Turtle goes to Reptile School every day of the week, including weekends.
He made one new friend each day.   How many friends did Tommy make in one week?

He made _____ friends. I know this because there are _____ days in a week.

<u>Extra:</u> What if he made one new friend every day for the first two weeks?

How many friends would he have made? _____

Name _____

More Than 10, Less Than 10

Look at the books on this page.

Do you think there are more than 10? _____

Do you think there are fewer than 10? _____

Now count the books to see if you were correct.

How many books were there? _____

Name _____

Hide-and-Seek Countdown

Jack Rabbit was playing "Hide and Seek." He was "It"! He had to count backwards from 10. Help Jack Rabbit by filling in the missing numbers.

10, 9 _____, 7, 6, _____, _____, 3, _____, 1

Extra: Help Jack Rabbit count backwards from 20 to 11.

20, _____, 18, 17, _____, 15, 14, _____, _____, 11

Name _____

Apple Colors

Apples can be red, yellow, or green. Ask your classmates which color apple they like best. Color in the boxes in the correct rows to show their answers.

Red																						
Yellow																						
Green																						

Which apple is the class favorite? _____

Name _____

Adding in Code

The number words below are missing vowels. Fill in the vowels to solve the code.

There were T H R _____ _____ plus F_____ _____ R apples on my tree.
I picked them so they would not fall.

When I added them up, my total was S _____ V _____ N.
That's how many apples I had in all!

Name _____

Pencil Puzzler

Katie Kangaroo started school with 6 new pencils. She lost 4.
Her friend Kenny gave her 2.

How many pencils does Katie have now? _____

Write your math equations here:

_____

_____

Name _____

One Bee in Our Classroom

Complete the poem by filling in the missing numbers.

1 bee in our classroom, and then there were 3.

Soon there were 5, straight from the hive.

Next there were _____.   That wasn't so fine.

And when the day ended, the total was _____.

Hint: Look for a pattern.

Name _____

Apple Problems

Nick needs to buy 8 apples. He needs the same number of red apples and green apples.
How many apples should he buy of each? Color in the apples to figure it out!

He needs _____ green apples and _____ red apples.

Extra: What if Nick needed 10, 12, 14, 16, or 18 apples?
Write your ideas on the back.

Name _____

Shapes All Around

Look around the classroom. What shapes do you see? Fill in each blank with an object.

The _____ is a rectangle.

The _____ is a square.

The _____ is a circle.

Shapes are everywhere!

Name _____

Red, Black, Snap, Clap

The beads on Beth's bracelet look like this: red, black, black, red, black, black, red, black, black, red.

What are the next three colors in the pattern? _____

Make the same pattern using the letters A and B. _____

<u>Extra:</u> Make the same pattern using snaps and claps.

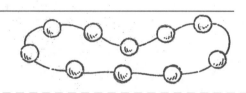

Name _____

The Last Leaves

From their home in a tree, Sid Squirrel said to his little sister Sally, "The oak tree has 5 leaves left. The maple tree has 3 more leaves than the oak.   How many leaves does the maple have?"

Draw a picture on the back to find the answer.

<u>Extra:</u> Write a math equation here: _____

How many in each group?   *What patterns do you see?*

Name _____

Falling Leaves

Solve this math riddle:

10 autumn leaves were hanging on a tree.
Along came the wind
and then there were 3.
How many leaves fell down on me? _____

Extra: Substitute a different number for 3.

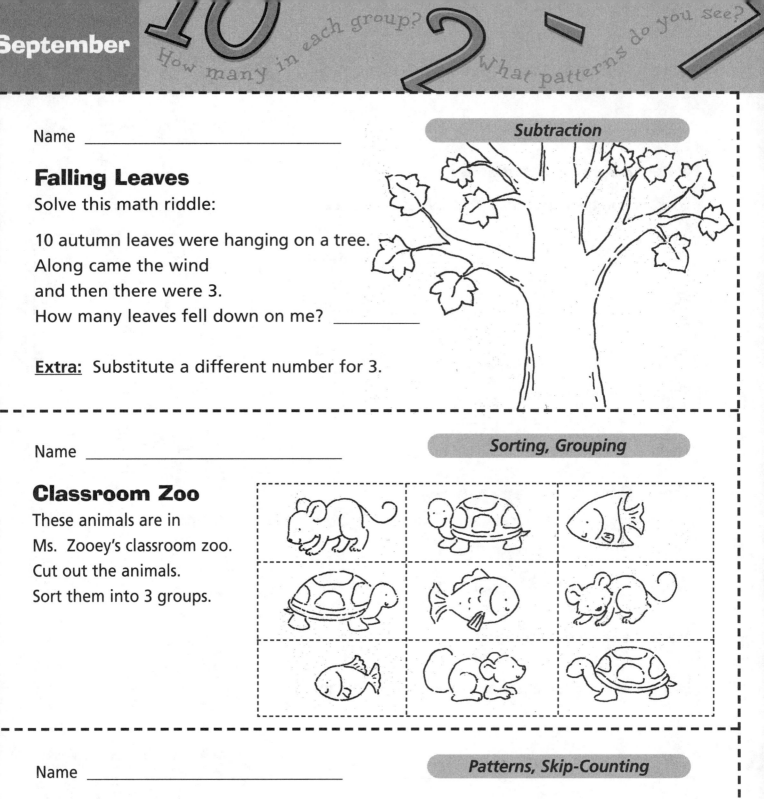

Name _____

Classroom Zoo

These animals are in
Ms. Zooey's classroom zoo.
Cut out the animals.
Sort them into 3 groups.

Name _____

Who Needs Glasses?

The children below had their eyes examined. How many eyes got checked? _____
Count by twos.

Name _____

Frog School

At Frog School, Croaker Frog and his friends sit on lily pads.
Are there enough lily pads for all the frogs in Croaker's class?
Draw lines to match the frogs with the lily pads.

How many frogs need lily pads? _____.

Big Foot

Benny Bear needed new shoes for the first day of school.
Here is his footprint.

?

Estimate how many inches his foot is from top to bottom.

_____

Now measure his foot. You can use linking cubes or a ruler.

How many inches is his foot? _____

Name _____

Mary Had a Little Puppy

Read the rhyme below.

Fill in the blanks with the correct words from the box.

above	followed	up	in	under

Mary had a little puppy

that _____ her to school.

The birds that flew _____ the puppy

said, "That's against the rule."

The puppy ran _____ the jungle gym.

Then he went _____ the classroom door.

He jumped _____ on the teacher's desk,

and barked and yipped and barked some more.

Extra

Color and cut out the figures below. Use them to act out the story.

15

Fall Leaf Patterns

Fred made a pattern using the leaves below. You can make patterns too. First, color the leaves as shown in the small boxes. Then color and cut out the bigger leaves. Use the leaves to make patterns.

Red	Orange	Yellow
maple leaf	oak leaf	elm leaf

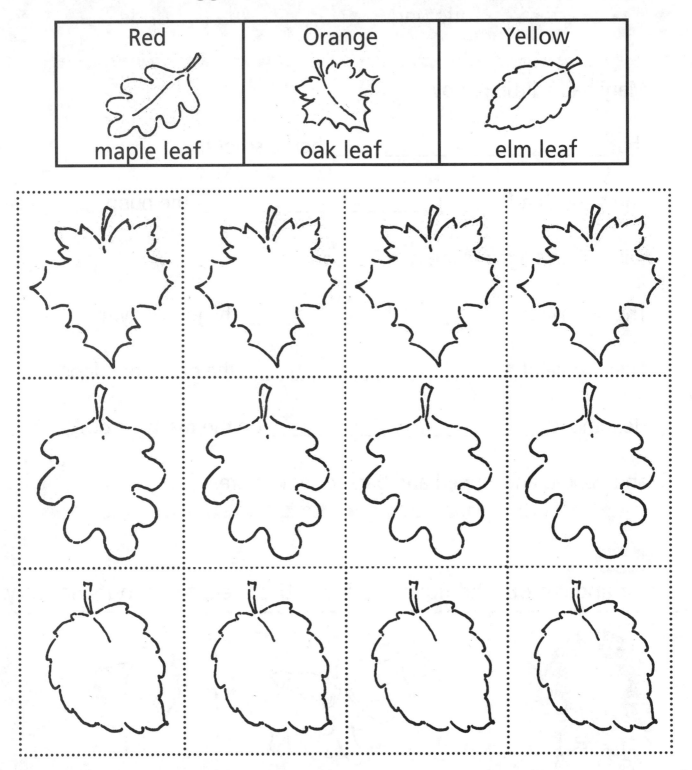

October

Name _____

Coin Detective

Solve this math rhyme.

Find a penny and a dime.

Find a nickel and a quarter.

Line them up from small to large.

Line them up in money order.

You can see it with your eyes.

The _____ is a funny size.

Explain your answer. _____

Name _____

Finger-Adding Game

Play this game with a partner. Say, "Ready, set, go." Then you and your partner both hold out some fingers on one hand. Try to get a sum of 5 when you add the fingers on both your hands. No talking!

How many tries does it take? _____

As a class, record the diffferent ways to make 5.

Extra: Try it with a different number, like 7 or 8!

How many in each group? What patterns do you see?

Name _____

Graphing, Comparing

Finding Favorite Colors

What is your favorite color? What about those of your classmates'?
Use color tiles to make a color graph like the one shown here.

Which color got the most votes? _____

How many votes did it get? _____

Which color got the fewest votes? _____

How many votes did it get?_____

red
blue
green
yellow
purple
pink

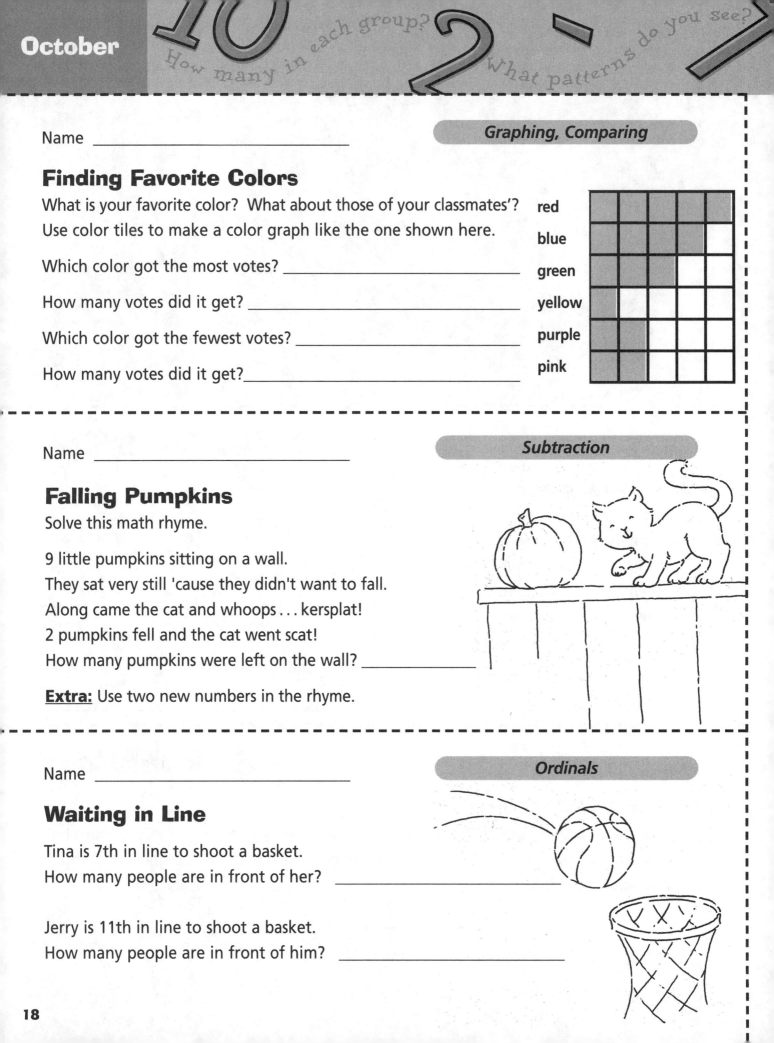

Name _____

Subtraction

Falling Pumpkins

Solve this math rhyme.

9 little pumpkins sitting on a wall.
They sat very still 'cause they didn't want to fall.
Along came the cat and whoops... kersplat!
2 pumpkins fell and the cat went scat!
How many pumpkins were left on the wall? _____

Extra: Use two new numbers in the rhyme.

Name _____

Ordinals

Waiting in Line

Tina is 7th in line to shoot a basket.
How many people are in front of her? _____

Jerry is 11th in line to shoot a basket.
How many people are in front of him? _____

Name _____

One and Only One

A silly king liked being number 1. So he made subtraction equations where all the answers were 1. He used the numbers 1, 2, 3, 4, and 5. Which equations did he make?

_____ – _____ = 1

_____ – _____ = 1

_____ – _____ = 1

_____ – _____ = 1

Name _____

Shape Hunters

Be a shape hunter. Fill in the blanks. Use the words in the box.

1. What shape is a can? _____

2. What shape is a ball? _____

3. What shape is an ice-cream cone? _____

4. What shape are number cubes? _____

5. What shape is a box? _____ or _____

cone
cube
cylinder
rectangular
sphere

Name _____

Poodles and Beagles

When Asheem went to the park, he counted 8 dogs. Some were poodles and some were beagles. How many poodles and how many beagles could there have been? Write as many number sentences as you can. Here is an example:

1 poodle + 7 beagles = 8 dogs in all

Use the other side or another sheet of paper to write your number sentence.

How many in each group?   What patterns do you see?

Name _____

Big Bad Wolf Math

The Big Bad Wolf is visiting the three little pigs. He is measuring their houses using his hands and feet. Circle "hand spans" or "giant steps" to show how he should measure these lengths.

1. The width of the third pig's door

2. The width of the third pig's house

3. The length from the first pig's house to the second pig's house

4. The width of the chimney opening

hand span   giant steps

hand span   giant steps

hand span   giant steps

hand span   giant steps

Name _____

National Cookie Month

October is National Cookie Month. Bethany and two friends baked 9 cookies. They divided the cookies into 3 equal piles.

How many cookies did each friend have?

_____

Extra: How many cookies would each friend have if they baked 12 cookies?

Name _____

Disappearing Counting Cubes

Play this game with a partner. Put 8 counters or cubes on a desk.

Close your eyes. Have your partner take away some of the counters.

Open your eyes. How many counters are left? _____

How many counters did your partner take? _____

Extra: Switch roles and play the game again!

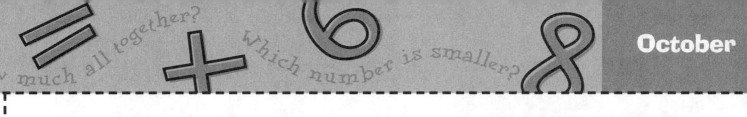

October

Name _____

Addition, Subtraction

Nan's Number Cubes

Nan threw two number cubes.
When she added the dots, she got 7.
One of the cubes looked like the one shown here.
What did the other cube look like?
Draw in the dots.

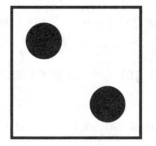

Name _____

Recognizing Shapes

Jack-O'-Lantern Designer

Make a jack-o-lantern face using 2 triangles, 2 squares
1 rectangle, and 1 circle.
Don't forget to draw teeth!

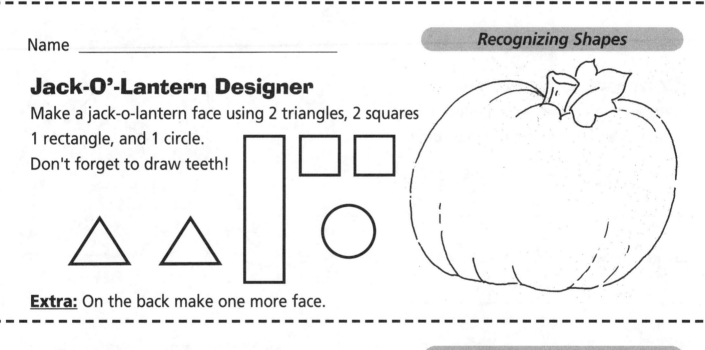

Extra: On the back make one more face.

Name _____

Adding Sums of 10

Three Halloween Kittens

Three black kittens weigh 10 pounds all together. One kitten weighs 4 pounds.
How much could each of the other two weigh?

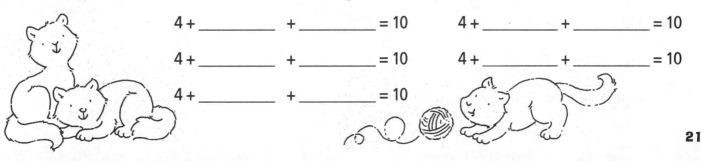

4 + _____ + _____ = 10   4 + _____ + _____ = 10

4 + _____ + _____ = 10   4 + _____ + _____ = 10

4 + _____ + _____ = 10

21

How many in each group? What patterns do you see?

Name _____

Addition

Trick or Treat?

Ashley and Ben went trick-or-treating.

Mrs. Story gave Ashley 3 treats. Mr. Story gave her 2 more.

Mrs. Story gave Ben 2 treats. Mr. Story gave him 3 more.

Did Ashley and Ben get the same number of treats? _____

Write the equations to show how you know:

_____   _____

Name _____

Subtraction

Comparing Costumes

Beth went trick-or-treating with 11 friends.

8 friends were wearing scary costumes.

How many were wearing other kinds of costumes?

_____

Write the equation to show how you know:

_____

Name _____

Graphing, Comparing

What's Your Costume?

Make a Halloween graph of the costumes in your class. Use these categories or ones you make up: **story character, funny, scary.** Draw your graph on another sheet of paper.

Which category has the most costumes? _____

How many does it have? _____

Which category has the fewest costumes? _____

A Friendly Scarecrow

This scarecrow has 2 birds on his right arm and 2 birds on his left arm.

How many birds are there in all?_____

Write the equation to show how you know:

_____

Extra

Now imagine there are 3 birds on each arm.

How many birds are there in total? _____

Imagine there are 4 birds on each arm.

How many birds are there in total? _____

What pattern do the numbers make? _____

_____

Sign Shape

Street signs come in different shapes. Use string to form the shapes below. Work with a partner. Answer the questions below about the shapes, too.

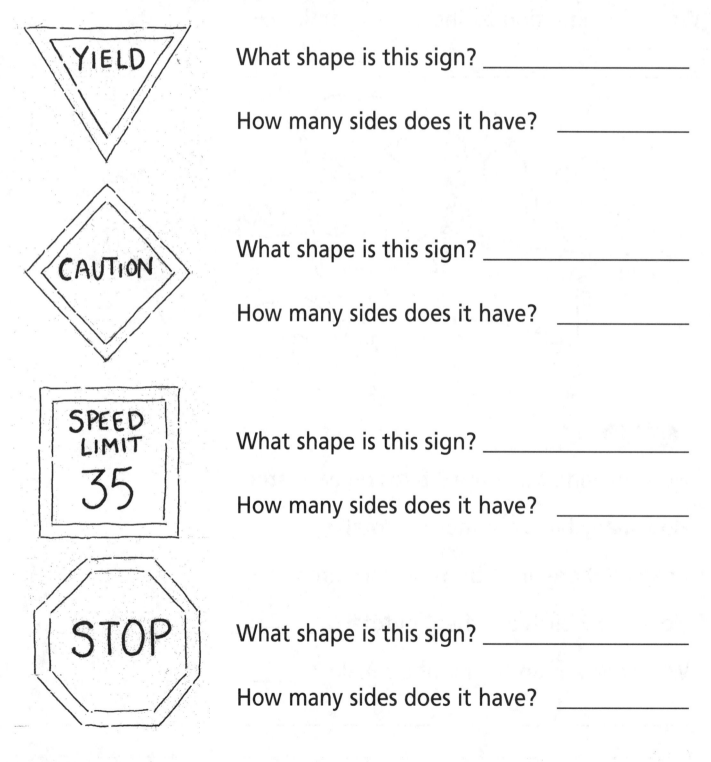

What shape is this sign? _____

How many sides does it have? _____

What shape is this sign? _____

How many sides does it have? _____

What shape is this sign? _____

How many sides does it have? _____

What shape is this sign? _____

How many sides does it have? _____

Name _____

Ladybug Dots

Every year, ladybugs hibernate when the weather gets cool. Count the dots on each ladybug wing. Then write an equation to show the total number of dots each ladybug has. The first one has been done for you.

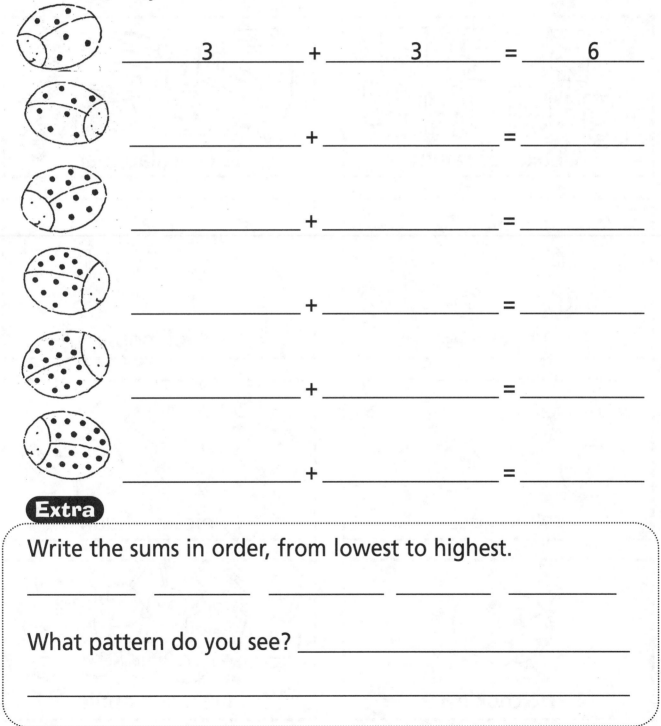

_____3_____ + _____3_____ = _____6_____

_____ + _____ = _____

_____ + _____ = _____

_____ + _____ = _____

_____ + _____ = _____

_____ + _____ = _____

Extra

Write the sums in order, from lowest to highest.

_____ _____ _____ _____ _____

What pattern do you see? _____

_____

Sorting Treats

Look at the Halloween treats below. Cut apart the boxes.
Then sort them into 2 piles. One pile is for numbers greater
than 10. The other pile is for numbers less than 10.

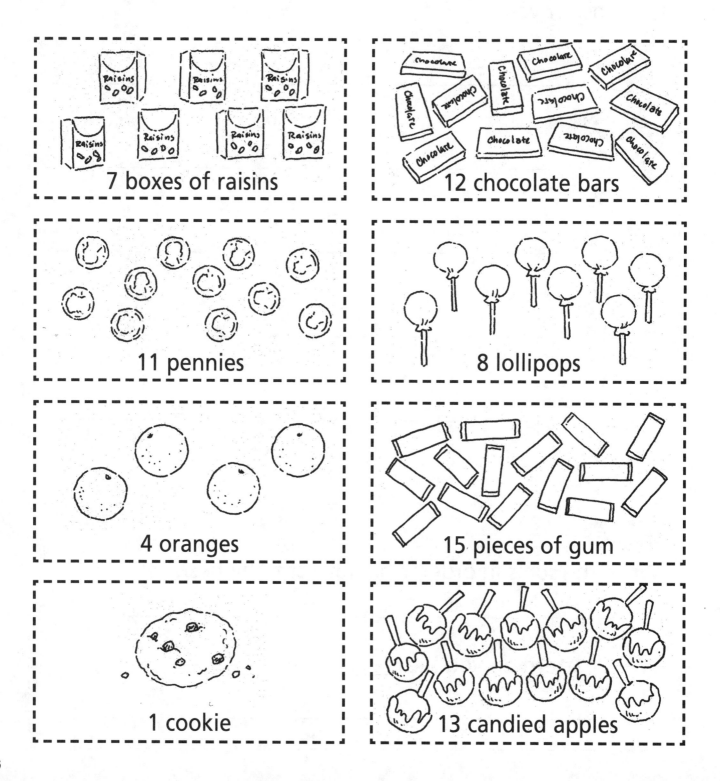

7 boxes of raisins

12 chocolate bars

11 pennies

8 lollipops

4 oranges

15 pieces of gum

1 cookie

13 candied apples

November

Name _____

Piggy Bank Puzzle

Tina heard her brother Joey counting coins.

Here's what Joey was saying: " . . . 30, 40, 50, 60 . . . "

What kind of coins was Joey counting? _____

Joey counted other coins. Tina heard, " . . . 30, 35, 40, 45 . . . "

What kind of coins was he counting now? _____

Name _____

Favorite Pet Tally

Elections are held in November. Have an election in your class. Ask your classmates to vote on which of the following animals they would like to have as a class mascot. Make tally marks next to each animal to show how your classmates voted.

dog _____ cat _____ bird _____ rabbit _____ other

Which animal was voted the mascot? _____

How many in each group? What patterns do you see?

Name _____

Playing in the Snow

A big snow storm dropped a lot of snow! Harry and his dog played in the snow for 6 days one week. Then they played for 7 days the next week. Use "doubles +1" to find out how many days they played in all. Write your equations on the lines. First write the doubles. Then the doubles plus one.

_____

_____

Name _____

Sorting, Classifying

ABC Sort

Look at the letters below. How could you sort them? Come up with categories and label them. Then list the letters for each. Show your work on the back of this paper, or on another sheet.

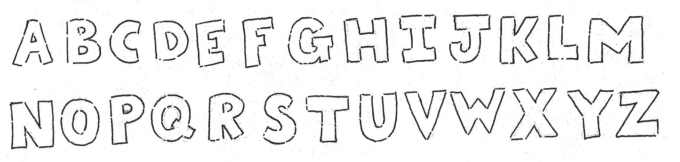

Name _____

Subtraction

How Many Birthdays?

In November, Timmy was 7 years old. How many more birthdays will Timmy have before he is 11, like his older brother? _____

Write the equations here to show how you know:

_____

Extra: When Timmy is 11, how old will his brother be? _____

Name _____

Game and Puzzle Week

The 4th week of November is "Game and Puzzle Week." To celebrate, see how many addition and subtraction equations you can make using only the numbers 2, 7, and 9.

_____

_____

_____

_____

Name _____

Birthday Riddle

Solve this math riddle.

On his birthday, David said:
"I am less than 10.
I am more than 4 + 4.
How old am I?"

_____

Name _____

Sledding Time

Eddie and his friends went sledding. There were 5 girls and 3 boys.
Make up an addition problem and a subtraction problem. Then solve them.

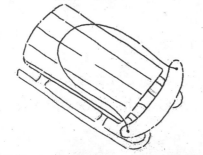

Addition: _____

_____

Subtraction: _____

_____

How many in each group? What patterns do you see?

Name _____

Wildlife Shelter

Josie volunteers at the wildlife shelter. In one year she helped 39 squirrels, 45 birds, and 28 gophers. Fill in the blanks with these numbers to show greater than and less than.

_____ > _____   _____ < _____

_____ > _____   _____ < _____

Extra: Read your results aloud to a partner.

Name _____

Mystery Drawing

Follow these directions to draw a mystery animal.
1. On another sheet of paper, draw a big circle in the middle.
2. To the left of the big circle, draw a little circle that touches the big circle.
3. Inside the little circle, draw a little square.
4. At the bottom of the big circle, draw two triangles that touch the circle.
5. To the right of the big circle, draw three long, thin, rectangles that touch the circle.
6. To the left of the little circle, draw a triangle that touches the circle and looks like a beak.
What did you draw?_____

Name _____

Gobbler Riddle

Solve this math riddle:
10 little gobblers sitting on a wall.
How many are big?
How many are small?

Write as many equations as you can that equal 10. Use the back of this sheet.

Example: $1 + 9 = 10$

Name _____

Thanksgiving Puzzler

Every year on Thanksgiving, someone at Teresa's house makes up a puzzle.
This year, Teresa said, "Which answer has the largest number: 11 - 3, 11 - 5, or 11 - 7?"
Try to solve Teresa's puzzle! Write your answer on the lines below
and explain it.

_____

_____

_____

Name _____

Mystery Holiday

Look at a calendar. Find the 11th month.

What is it? _____

Now find the last Thursday of that month.

What is the date? _____

Which holiday do we celebrate on that day?

_____

Name _____

Mashed, Baked, or Fried?

What kinds of potatoes do you and your classmates like to eat on Thanksgiving? Draw a tally
mark next to each potato dish. If the dish is not listed, draw a tally mark next to "other."

mashed _____   baked _____

fried _____   other _____

Count up the tally marks for each potato.
Which potato dish is the class favorite? _____

Scavenger Hunt

Cut out the acorn ruler on this page.
Each acorn is 1– inch long.
Use the acorn ruler for this scavenger hunt.

1. Find an object that is 2 inches long.

_____

2. Find an object that is 4 inches long.

_____

3. Find an object that is 6 inches long.

_____

4. Find an object that is 8 inches long.

_____

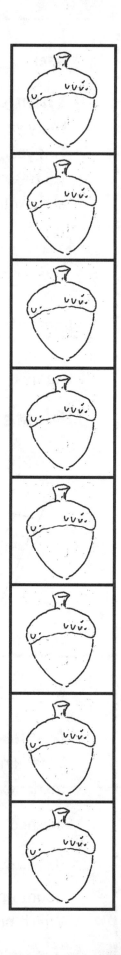

Name _____

Collecting Food

Lan's class collected food to give to needy families on Thanksgiving. Cut out the cans below. Sort them into three groups. On another sheet of paper, make a bar graph to show how many cans are in each group. Name the groups.

Name _____

Money Matters

Alex asked his little brother Billy to trade piggy banks.

Alex's bank has these coins: Billy's has these coins:

Extra

Do you think this is a fair trade? _____

Test your answer:

Add up Alex's coins: _____

Add up Billy's coins: _____

Write the totals in this Greater Than/Less Than equation:

_____ > _____

Who has more money? _____

Penguin Family on Parade

The penguin family is part of the winter parade. They need to line up from shortest to tallest. Give them a hand! Use a ruler to measure each penguin. Label each penguin with its height. Then write the name of each penguin in size order, from smallest to tallest.

Paul	**Peter**	**Patty**	**Petunia**
Height:	Height:	Height:	Height:
_____	_____	_____	_____
inches	inches	inches	inches

Size Order:

_____   _____   _____   _____

(smallest)   (tallest)

Thanksgiving Play

The class put on a Thanksgiving play. Two children were playing Pilgrims. The total number of children playing Native Americans was 2 more than the number of children playing Pilgrims. Draw Pilgrim or Native American costumes on the correct number of children.

Extra

How many children were in the play? _____

How many children were not in the play? _____

December

Name _____

Addition, Subtraction

On and Off the Bus

Solve this rhyming math riddle:

4 kids are riding on the bus.
2 kids get off, 3 more get on.
The wheels turn, the horn goes beep,
They sing a song to the driver, Ron.

How many kids sing to the driver? _____

Write your equation. _____

Name _____

Adding and Subtracting with 0

Magic Tricks

Jerry did magic tricks at his birthday party. Write equations
for the tricks below. Use 0 (zero) in each equation.

Trick 1: Jerry put 6 rabbits in a
hat and made them disappear.

Trick 2: Jerry had no birds. He stuck his
hand in his sleeve and pulled out 5 birds.

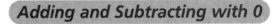

_____   _____

37

Name _____

Beehive Hexagons

A cell in a beehive has 6 sides. A shape with 6 sides is called a hexagon.
Find a yellow hexagon among the Pattern Blocks in your classroom.
Then use the other Pattern Block shapes to cover the yellow hexagon
in as many ways as you can. Draw or trace the ways on another
piece of paper.

Example:

How many different ways can you cover the hexagon?

_____

Name _____

Basketball Time

Help Jen get ready for her basketball game.
Fill in the blanks below with 1 minute, 5 minutes and 2 hours.

When Jen woke up, she brushed her teeth for _____. She put on all her

basketball clothes in _____. Then she headed out the door for her game.

"I'll be back in _____," she shouted to her brother.

Name _____

Barn Owl's Mistake

In the cold winter barn, Barn Owl said to the horses,
"I have found a good way to add numbers in my head. Listen to this:

If 4 + 4 = 8, then 4 + 5 = 7. If 6 + 6 = 12, then 6 + 7 = 11."

Put a star by the wrong answers. Write the correct ones here: _____ , _____

What is Barn Owl doing wrong? How can doubles help you add? Write your ideas on the back.

Name _____

Cold Fingers and Toes

Draw a picture on the back of this sheet of 4 children playing in the snow, building snow people. When they were finished, the fingers and toes of all the children were icy cold.

How many cold fingers and toes were there in all?

_____

Use skip counting or multiplication to show your answer.

_____

Name _____

Two by Two

If your class lined up in 2's, would everyone have a partner? Count everyone's name tag, or line up, to find out.

Is there an even or an odd number of kids in your class? _____

How do you know? _____

_____

Name _____

The Goldfish Gift

Greg wanted to buy a goldfish for his friend Graham. The goldfish cost 25¢. Show all the different ways Greg could pay for the goldfish using coins. Draw or write your answers below. Use the back if you need more room.

_____   _____

_____   _____

How many in each group? What patterns do you see?

Name _____

Exactly in the Middle

Solve this math riddle:

A group of kids went ice skating.
There were between 60 and 70 kids.
The exact number was exactly in the middle.
How many children went ice skating?

_____

Hint: You can use a number line to find out.

Name _____

Pie Slices

Polly was cutting peach pies.

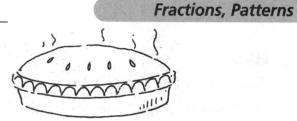

She cut one pie in 2 equal slices, or halves. How many cuts did she make? _____

She cut one pie into 4 equal slices, or fourths. How many cuts did she make? _____
Hint: draw pies on the back of this sheet to help you.

Extra: She cut one pie into 6 equal slices, or sixths. How many cuts did she make? _____

Name _____

A Nickel a Month

Most people keep their money in a bank account. The money earns "interest."
This means that the bank adds money to the money in the bank account.

If the bank adds 5¢ every month for 1 year, how much extra money would there be?

_____

Hint: You can skip count or write the multiplication equation to find the answer.

Name _____

Thumbprints and Hand Spans

Suppose you used your thumbprint or your hand span to measure your desk.

Which measurement would be larger? _____

Use your thumbprint to measure your desk.

How many thumbprints long is your desk? _____

Now use your hand span to measure your desk.

How many hand-spans long is your desk? _____

Name _____

A Wingful of Books

Over the long holiday vacation, Owl took out a wingful of books from the library.
She read 7 the first week. How many did she have left to read?

What information would you need to answer this question?

_____

Make up a number of books for Owl to take out of the library.
Write and solve your equation now.

_____

Name _____

Holiday Piggy Bank

Franny Frog was saving pennies to buy holiday gifts.
On the 1st day she saved 1 penny. On the 2nd day, she saved 2 pennies.
On the 3rd day, she saved 3 pennies.

How many pennies did she save on the 4th day? _____

How many pennies did she save on the 5th day? _____

How many pennies did she save in all? _____

How many in each group? What patterns do you see?

Name _____

Graphing, Comparing

Family Time at Holiday Time

Holiday time is family time. Everyone's family is special.
How many people are in your family? On another sheet
of paper, make a bar graph, like the one shown here.
Color in the squares to show how many people are in
your classmates' families.

Which bar on the graph is longest? _____

What does this tell you? Write your answer on the back.

People in our Families					
2 people					
3 people					
4 people					
5 people					
6 people					
7 people					
8 people					

Name _____

Adding Sums of 10

Holiday Cookies

Jack Rabbit and his sister made holiday cookies. Some were carrot cookies. Some were sugar
cookies. There were 10 cookies in all. How many cookies could they have made of
each kind? Write your answers in equations.

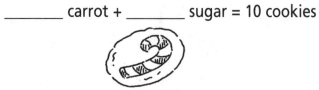

_____ carrot + _____ sugar = 10 cookies   _____ carrot + _____ sugar = 10 cookies

_____ carrot + _____ sugar = 10 cookies   _____ carrot + _____ sugar = 10 cookies

Keep going! Write more equations on the back.

Snowflakes on Mittens

Estimate how many snowflakes are on each mitten. _____   _____

For the first mitten, skip count by 2s
to find out. (You can circle groups of 2.) _____

For the second mitten, skip count by 5s
to check your answer. (You can circle groups of 5.) _____

Extra

Would snowflakes really wait for you to count? _____

Explain your answer: _____

Quilt Colors

Grandpa Squirrel wants to make Baby Squirrel a warm winter quilt. Here is the quilt pattern he's using:

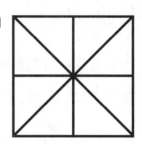

He'll be using 4 red triangles and 4 blue triangles. Find different ways to make the quilt.   Color the triangles below.

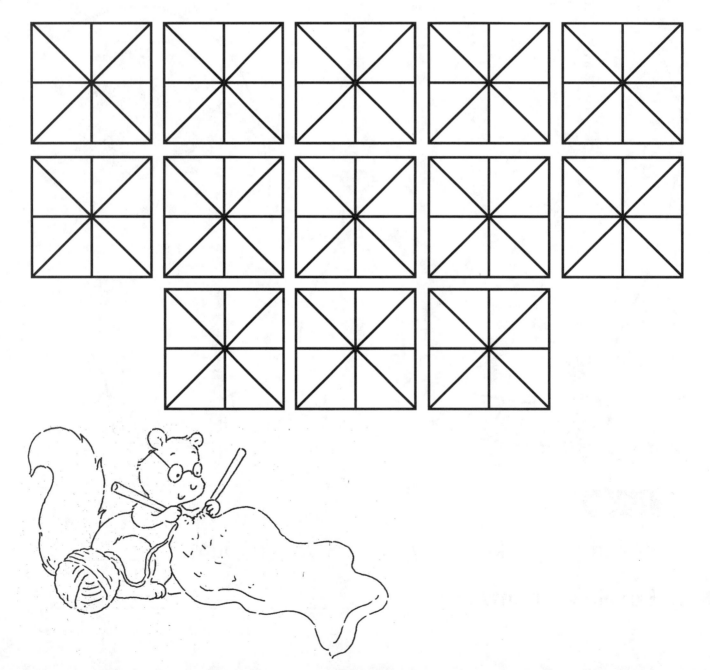

Name _____

Cabin in the Snow

Fill in the blanks in the poem. Look at the pictures to help you.

Little Cabin in the Snow

_____ – sided snowflakes, soft and cold.

_____ – sided cabin, warm and bright.

_____ – sided doorway, where Grandma stands

with steamy, round pancakes that taste just right.

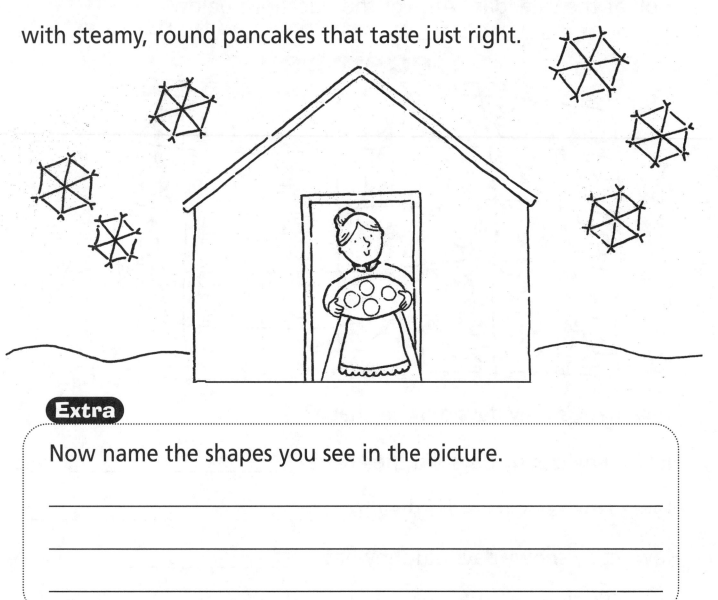

Extra

Now name the shapes you see in the picture.

_____

_____

_____

December Weather

In December, Mrs. Monroe's class drew the weather on a calendar. Each kind of weather has a picture:

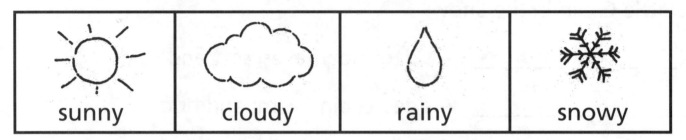

| sunny | cloudy | rainy | snowy |

Look at the calendar. Answer the questions below.

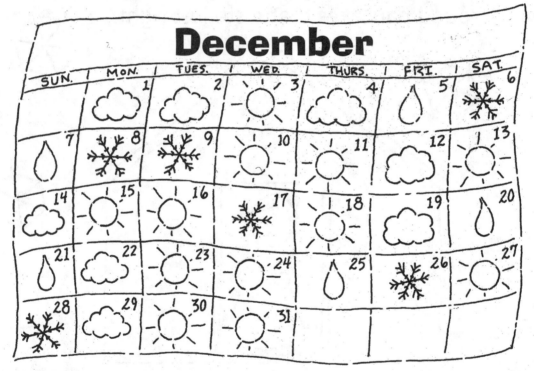

How many sunny days did they have?_____

How many cloudy days did they have?_____

How many rainy days did they have?_____

How many snowy days did they have?_____

Which kind of weather did they have the most?_____

January

Name _____

Muffins by the Dozen

After sledding, Bo and his friends went home to eat muffins and drink cocoa.
There were a dozen muffins to start. Bo and his friends gobbled down 5.

How many were left? _____

Write an equation to show how you figured out the answer.

_____

Name _____

Rolling & Stacking

Read the sentences below. Figure out who's talking.
Is it a sphere? A cylinder? A cube? Fill in the blanks.

"I can roll." _____   "I can roll, too." _____

"I can stack." _____   "I can stack, too. _____

How many in each group?

What patterns do you see?

Name _____

Penguin School

In the winter, the Penguin School is not open on weekends.
Polly Penguin learns one new thing every day of school.

How many new things does she learn in 1 week? _____

Explain your answer: _____

Extra: What if Polly learns one new thing each day of school for 2 weeks?

　　　How many new things would she learn then? _____

Name _____

Guess My Number

Gordo Gecko said, "Guess my number.　It is between 32 and 37."

Which number could it be?

_____

His number was 33. Did Gordo give a good enough hint? _____

What other hints could he have given? _____

Name _____

Hibernation Breaks

In winter, chipmunks hibernate. At times they might wake up. Every
time Chad Chipmunk wakes up, his mother asks him a math problem.
Help Chad answer these math questions so he can go back to sleep.

Which has more flat sides—a cylinder or a cube? _____

How many more? _____

Hint: Compare a cube and a cylinder to solve the problem.

Name _____

Danny Duck's Dinner

Danny Duck went to buy some food for dinner.   He had 10¢.

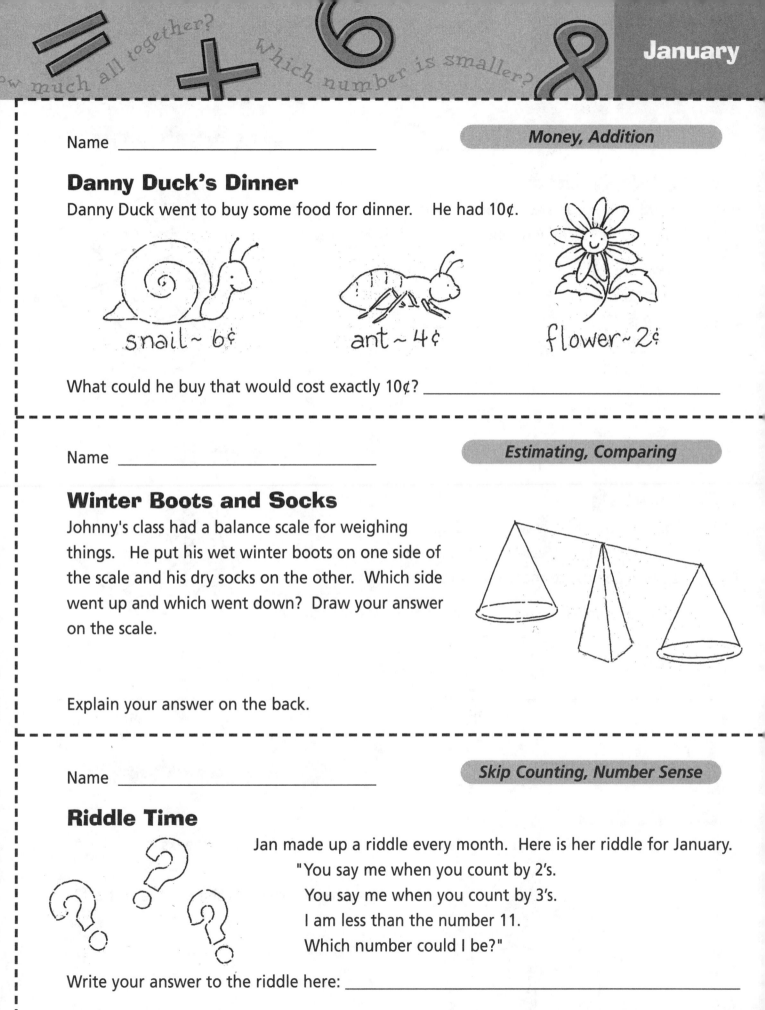

snail ~ 6¢   ant ~ 4¢   flower ~ 2¢

What could he buy that would cost exactly 10¢? _____

Name _____

Winter Boots and Socks

Johnny's class had a balance scale for weighing things.   He put his wet winter boots on one side of the scale and his dry socks on the other. Which side went up and which went down? Draw your answer on the scale.

Explain your answer on the back.

Name _____

Riddle Time

Jan made up a riddle every month. Here is her riddle for January.

"You say me when you count by 2's.

You say me when you count by 3's.

I am less than the number 11.

Which number could I be?"

Write your answer to the riddle here: _____

49

How many in each group? What patterns do you see?

Name _____

MLK Jr.'s Birthday

Martin Luther King, Jr.'s actual birthday falls in January between the numbers 14 and 19. Figure out which day it is with these clues.

It's an odd number.
It's lower than 16.
Which day is it? _____

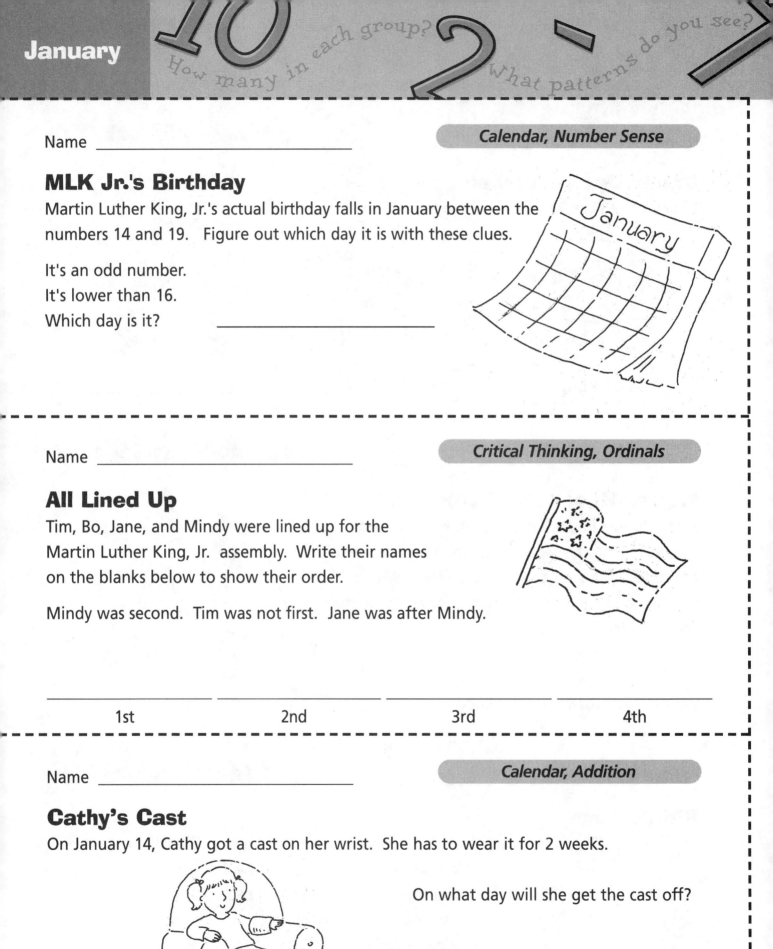

Name _____

All Lined Up

Tim, Bo, Jane, and Mindy were lined up for the Martin Luther King, Jr. assembly. Write their names on the blanks below to show their order.

Mindy was second. Tim was not first. Jane was after Mindy.

_____ _____ _____ _____
1st   2nd   3rd   4th

Name _____

Cathy's Cast

On January 14, Cathy got a cast on her wrist. She has to wear it for 2 weeks.

On what day will she get the cast off?

_____

Hint: Look at a calendar to help you.

Name _____

Cool Calculations

Penny Pig's favorite numbers were 3 and 4.   She tried to make different numbers appear on her calculator by pressing the 3, the 4, the plus sign, and the equal sign in different orders.

How did she get to 16? Write the equation here.

_____

How did she get to 11? Write the equation here.

_____

Name _____

Bear Family Quilts

Baby Bear's quilt looks like this:

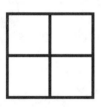

Mama Bear's quilt is bigger and looks like this:

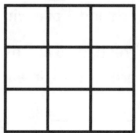

Papa Bear's quilt is the biggest. On another sheet, draw what Papa Bear's quilt would look like.
Extra: Use color tiles to make all the quilts.

Name _____

Temperature Matcheroo

Every morning, Jimmy looked at a thermometer outside his window. The thermometer measured the temperature. Draw a line to match these temperatures with the seasons.

90°	fall
70°	summer
50°	winter
30°	spring

Hint: Remember which seasons are usually warmest and coolest

How many in each group? What patterns do you see?

Name _____

Favorite Number Graph

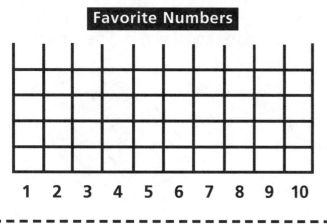

Favorite Numbers

1 2 3 4 5 6 7 8 9 10

Ask your classmates to pick their favorite numbers between 1 and 10. On another sheet of paper make a bar graph, like the one here, to record their answer. Draw one X in the column for each choice.

What did you learn from the graph? Did more people pick even numbers or odd numbers? Write what you learned on the back.

Name _____

Squirrel Math

Sally Squirrel had 25 acorns. She made 3 piles. She made 2 piles with 10 acorns each and 1 pile with 5 acorns.   Sally said, "10 + 10 + 5 = 25."

Sidney Squirrel had 36 acorns. He brought them to Sally. Sally made 4 piles. How many acorns were in each pile?

Pile #1 _____ Pile #2 _____ Pile # 3 _____ Pile #4 _____

What do you think Sally said? _____

Name _____

Pie Fight

To celebrate National Pie Day, the circus clowns made 26 cream pies. They threw 11 at each other in a pie fight. They ate the rest.

How many pies did they eat? _____

Write an equation to show how you got your answer.

_____

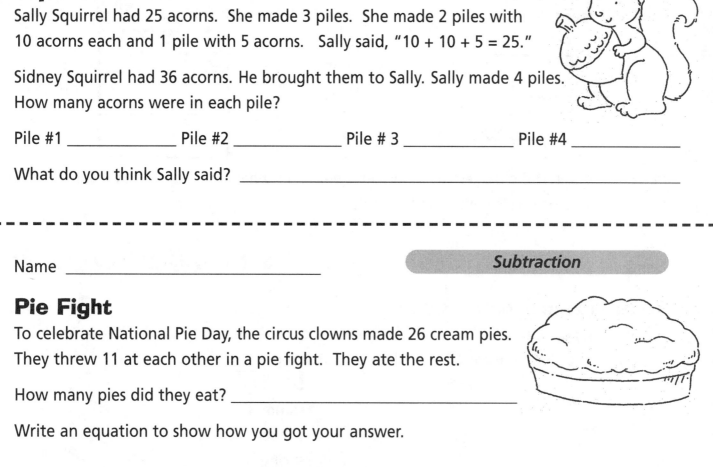

Name _____

National Popcorn Day

National Popcorn Day is at the end of January. It is the same day as Super Bowl Sunday. Bring in some wrapped popcorn kernels. Fill a tablespoon with popcorn kernels. Estimate how many kernels are on the spoon.

Write your estimate here: _____

Now count them. Write the exact number here: _____

Show the two numbers you wrote in a greater than/less than equation. _____

Name _____

Coin Puzzler

January 29 is National Puzzle Day. Solve this riddle to celebrate.

<u>3</u> shiny coins inside the piggy bank
are worth <u>16</u> cents. Clank, clank, clank.

What coins are in the bank? _____ _____ _____

<u>Extra:</u> Now substitute <u>4</u> and <u>26</u> for the numbers in the poem. Write your answer on the back.

Scarf Patterns

Marla's grandmother is knitting three scarves. Help her finish each scarf by continuing each pattern.

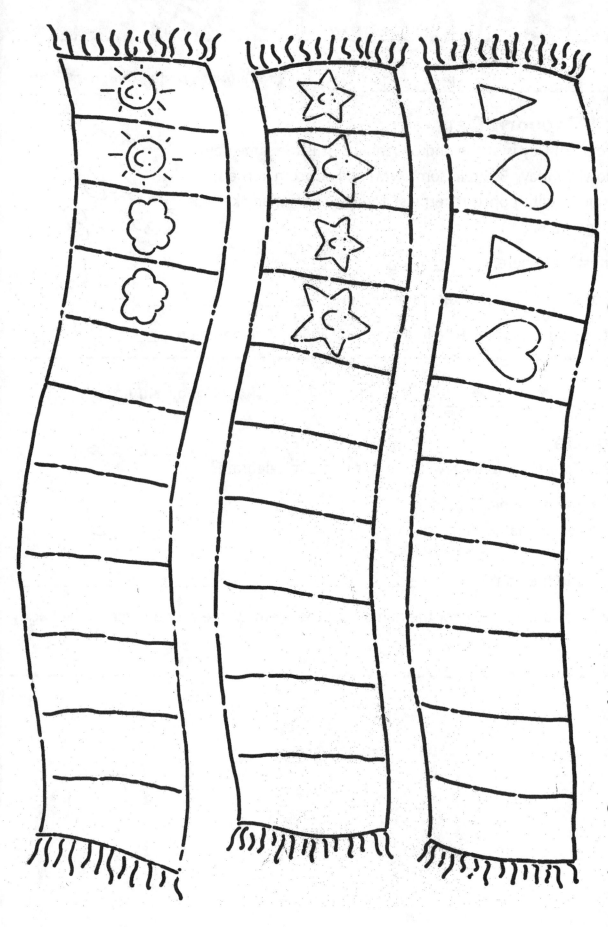

What to Wear?

Tina had 2 pairs of pants. One was black. One was white. She had 3 sweaters. They were red, yellow, and blue. Color in the clothes below. Cut them out. Make as many different outfits as you can.

How many did you make? _____

Do you think Tina would be late for
school if she tried on all your outfits? _____

Name _____

Dalmatian Spots

Dana's Dalmatian has lots of spots.

How many do you think it has?_____

Check your estimate by skip counting by fives.
(Circle groups of five.)

How many spots does it have?_____

February

Name _____

Money, Addition

Chinese New Year

For Chinese New Year, some children receive money in red envelopes.
Which would you rather have in your envelope—3 quarters or 7 dimes?

I would rather have _____

Explain your answer. _____

_____

Name _____

Time

Ground Hog Day

The ground hog woke up at 10:00. Two hours later,
he popped his head out of his hole to look at his shadow.

What time did the ground hog check his shadow?

_____

How many in each group? What patterns do you see?

Name _____

Black History Month

George has 39 stamps in his stamp collection. He bought 3 new stamps that show "Black Heroes in History." George said, "Now I have 43 stamps in all."

Was George correct? Circle Yes or No.   **YES**   **NO**

Explain your answer. _____

_____

Name _____

Estimating Weight and Length

Pennies and Paper Clips

On the 100th day of school, Joan's class weighed 100 pennies and 100 paper clips.

Which do you think was heavier? _____

Then they put the 100 pennies in one line and the 100 paper clips in another.

Which line do you think was longer? _____

Hint: Get a few pennies and a few paper clips. Experiment to figure out the answers.

Name _____

Skip Counting, Patterns

100th Day of School

Read this math riddle:

To celebrate the 100th day, count to 100 by 10s.
If you say all the numbers out loud, estimate how many will you say?

Write the numbers you used to count to 100 by 10s. _____

How many numbers did you write? _____

Talk with a classmate about the patterns you see.

Name _____

Thirsty, Anyone?

A cup of hot cocoa is perfect on a cold winter day. But lemonade hits the spot in the summer, . What is your favorite drink? What drinks do your classmates like? On another sheet of paper, make a bar graph to record their choices.

Which drink is the most popular? _____

How can you tell? _____

Name _____

Bear Riddles

Solve these riddles about bears. Write the bear name on the lines.

My fur is white. I live in the Arctic.
The first letter of my name is the 16th letter of the alphabet.
What kind of bear am I? _____ _____ _____ _____ _____ bear

My fur is brown. I am one of the biggest bears in the world.
The first letter of my name is the 7th letter of the alphabet.
What kind of bear am I? _____ _____ _____ _____ _____ _____ _____ bear

---

Name _____

Pictures of Presidents

Solve this math riddle.

I have 2 bills that show President Lincoln's head.
I have 3 bills with Washington on them instead.

How much money do I have? _____

Write an equation to show how you know.

Name _____

Who Is Older?

Josh and Ashley turned 7 years old this year. Ashley's birthday is in January on Martin Luther King, Jr. Day. Josh's birthday is in February on Valentine's Day.

Who is older? _____

Explain your answer. _____

_____

Name _____

Sloppy Winter Boots

Solve this math riddle.

12 sloppy winter boots
are sitting by the door.
How many children are
sipping cocoa on the floor? _____

Hint: Use manipulatives to help solve the riddle.

Extra: Now 16 boots are by the door. How many children are there? _____

Name _____

Odd + Odd

Jerry added two odd numbers and came up with 8.

What numbers did Jerry use? Write 2 equations to show your ideas.

_____   _____

Jerry tried adding two odd numbers to come up with an odd number. Explain why it didn't work.

Name _____

Multiplication

So Many Stamps!

Sandy is sending a very large Valentine's Day
card to a friend. To mail it, she needs 12 stamps.
She is arranging the stamps in rows. Each row
has the same number of stamps. How many
different arrangements can she make? Try it!
On the back, or on another sheet of paper, draw
a picture to show the ways you could arrange
the stamps in equal rows.

Name _____

Addition, Multiplication

Valentine Count

Mario received 6 valentines. Barb received 6 valentines. Maria received 6 valentines, too.

How many valentines did they get in all? _____

Explain how you figured out the answer. _____

_____

Name _____

Number Sense, Calendar

Special Birthday

Justin's brother was 20 years old on the day after February 19 in the year 2000.
Why was this birthday special? These questions will help you.

Which month is February? (1st, 2nd, 3rd, ...?) _____ Which day is his birthday? __

How old was he?_____ In which year was he this age?_____

What do the numbers have in common?_____

Extra: What would be a special birthday in the year 1999? Write your idea on the back.

Name _____

Measuring His Shadow

When the ground hog came out to check his shadow, the inchworm said the shadow was 10 inchworms long. The frog said the shadow was 5 frogs long. Cut out the inchworms, the frogs, and the shadow to find out.

How many inchworms equal the shadow? _____

How many frogs equal the length of the shadow? _____

Who was right? _____

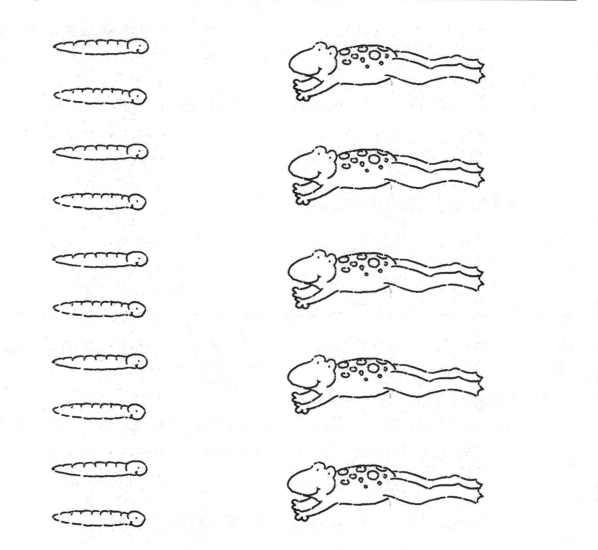

Name _____

Snow-Print Detective

Sally dropped a big box in the snow. Lots of things fell out.
Look at each object. Below it, write which kind of print it would
make in the snow. Use the shape words in the box.

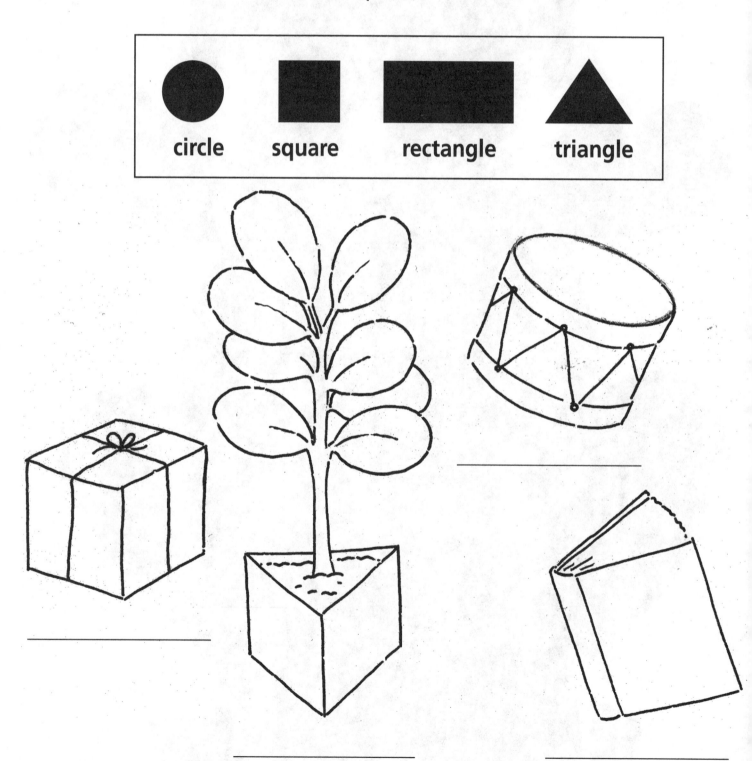

circle   square   rectangle   triangle

Name _____

Valentine Symmetry

Janis folded all her valentines in half. Some were symmetrical.
That means, one half matches the other half. Some valentines
were not symmetrical.

Cut out the valentine shapes below. Fold them in half
so you make a crease that runs from top to bottom.
Which ones are symmetrical?

_____   _____

_____   _____

Fold the symmetrical shapes in half so that
you make a crease running from left to right.

Which shape is symmetrical this way? _____

Valentine Stickeroo

Martha Mule made a valentine for Max Mule. She had 4 stickers in 2 different colors. How many ways could she arrange the stickers on the card?

Here are the stickers:

Here are some blank cards:
Draw stickers in the squares of the cards to
show how Marla could arrange them.

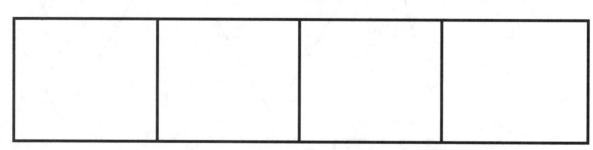

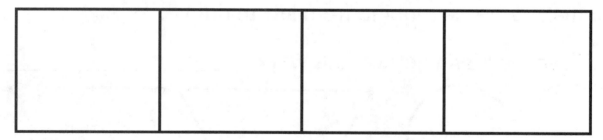

Are there more ways? Draw them on the back.

Picking Out Patterns

On the 100th day of school, everyone in Pat's class picked out patterns on the 100 Chart. Look at the chart below.

1	2	3	4	5	6	7	8	9	10
11	12	13	14	15	16	17	18	19	20
21	22	23	24	25	26	27	28	29	30
31	32	33	34	35	36	37	38	39	40
41	42	43	44	45	46	47	48	49	50
51	52	53	54	55	56	57	58	59	60
61	62	63	64	65	66	67	68	69	70
71	72	73	74	75	76	77	78	79	80
81	82	83	84	85	86	87	88	89	90
91	92	93	94	95	96	97	98	99	100

Find and finish the pattern starting with 2, 12, 22,...

_____

Find and finish the pattern starting with 100, 90, 80,...

_____

Find and finish the pattern starting with 97, 87, 77,...

_____

Find and finish the pattern starting with 11, 22, 33,...

_____

Presidents' Day Problem

The first 18 Presidents of the United States are listed below.
They are shown in order.

1. George Washington (1789–1797)
2. John Adams (1797–1801)
3. Thomas Jefferson (1801–1809)
4. James Madison (1809–1817)
5. James Monroe (1817–1825)
6. John Quincy Adams (1825–1829)
7. Andrew Jackson (1829–1837)
8. Martin Van Buren (1837–1841)
9. William Henry Harrison (1841)
10. John Tyler (1841–1845)
11. James Knox Polk (1845–1849)
12. Zachary Taylor (1849–1850)
13. Millard Fillmore (1850–1853)
14. Franklin Pierce (1853–1857)
15. James Buchanan (1857–1861)
16. Abraham Lincoln (1861–1865)
17. Andrew Johnson (1865–1869)
18. Ulysses S. Grant (1869–1877)

1. Which President was Washington? **The 1st**

2. Which President was Lincoln? _____

3. Which President came before Lincoln? _____

4. Which President came after Lincoln? _____

5. How many Presidents were there <u>between</u> Washington and Lincoln? _____

March

Name _____

Colorful Kites

It was a windy March day. Some kids in the park were flying kites.

• The yellow kite was the highest.

• The red kite was between the yellow kite and the blue kite.

• The green kite was the lowest.

On another sheet of paper, draw a picture and color it to show the positions of the kites.

Name _____

What's for Breakfast?

The first week of March is National School Breakfast Week. Take a survey of your class to find out each classmate's favorite breakfast. Show the results on a graph. Model your graph after the one shown here .

Which breakfast was the most popular? _____

How could you tell? _____

Cereal			
Pancakes			
Eggs			
Oatmeal			
French Toast			

How many in each group?

What patterns do you see?

Name _____

The Three Bears' Orange Juice

The three bears are coming out of hibernation. They are going for a walk.
Look at the thermoses below. Papa Bear's thermos holds 8 cups of orange juice.

Estimate how many cups Mama Bear's thermos holds.

_____ cups

Estimate how many cups Baby Bear's thermos holds.

_____ cups

Explain your estimates on the back.

Name _____

Money Riddle

A second-grade class is having a spring taco sale to raise money. Tim has 10¢
to spend on tacos. Jen has 5¢ more than Tim. How much money does Jen have? _____

Write an equation to show how you figured out the answer.

_____

Ralph has 2¢ more than Jen. How much money does Ralph have? _____

Write another equation to show the answer. _____

Name _____

The Shrinking Teddy Bear

Pat's teddy bear is shrinking! On Monday, the bear's waist measured 20 inches around.
On Tuesday, it measured 18 inches. On Wednesday, it measured 16 inches.

At this rate, what would it measure on Thursday? _____

What would it measure on Friday? _____

What would it measure on Saturday? _____

Why do you think the bear was shrinking? _____

Name _____

Addition, Subtraction

Finding Gold

March 17 is St. Patrick's Day. Leprechauns are in Irish folklore. A leprechaun found 7 gold coins under a bush. He found 8 more at the end of a rainbow. He spent 3 of the coins on a tiny hammer.

How many coins does he have left to spend? _____

Write 2 number sentences to show how you figured out the answer.

_____

_____

Name _____

Comparing, Greater Than/Less Than

Leprechaun Gold

Larry Leprechaun put his gold coins on the right side of the balance scale. Lizzy Leprechaun put hers on the left side. Here is how the balance scale looked.

Count Larry's gold coins. Write the number here: _____

Now draw in the number of gold coins Lizzy might have had.

Write a greater than/less than equation to show your ideas: _____ > _____

Name _____

Estimating, Measuring Length

Leprechaun Steps

On another sheet of paper, draw what you imagine a leprechaun footprint might look like. Cut it out. How many leprechaun footprints would it be from your desk to the door?

Write your estimate here: _____
Now use your cutout to measure the distance.

Write how many footprints it really is from your desk to the door. _____

71

How many in each group? What patterns do you see?

Name _____

Place Value, Greater Than/Less Than

Who Won?

Jane's team played Kira's team in basketball. Jane's team had a score of 6 tens and 4 ones.

What was their score? _____

Kira's team had a score of 4 tens and 6 ones.

What was their score? _____

Write the numbers in this greater than/less than equation: _____ > _____

Which team won? _____

Name _____

Using a Calculator, Counting by 5's

Dog Calculations

Sara pressed 5 + on her calculator. Her dog started thumping his paw on the + key. He pressed it 4 more times. Fill in the blanks below to show the numbers that came up on the calculator.

5, _____ , _____ , _____ , _____

You will need to use calculator. Press 5 +.
Press the + key again and again.

Name _____

Subtraction

Lost-and-Found Mystery

Daniel counted clothes at the school Lost and Found. In the winter, he counted 26 items. In the spring, there were only 4 items. How many more items were in Lost and Found in the winter than in the spring?

Write an equation to show your answer. _____

Extra: Why do you think there were more items in the Lost and Found in the winter? Explain your idea on the back.

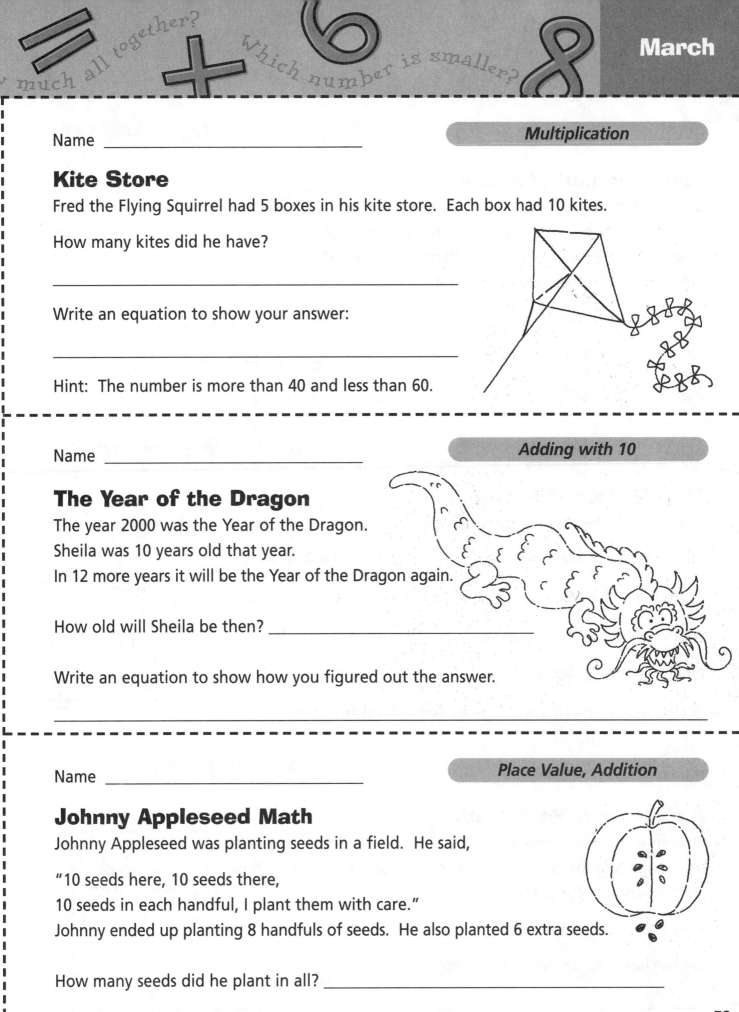

Name _____

Kite Store

Fred the Flying Squirrel had 5 boxes in his kite store. Each box had 10 kites.

How many kites did he have?

_____

Write an equation to show your answer:

_____

Hint: The number is more than 40 and less than 60.

Name _____

Adding with 10

The Year of the Dragon

The year 2000 was the Year of the Dragon.
Sheila was 10 years old that year.
In 12 more years it will be the Year of the Dragon again.

How old will Sheila be then? _____

Write an equation to show how you figured out the answer.

_____

Name _____

Place Value, Addition

Johnny Appleseed Math

Johnny Appleseed was planting seeds in a field. He said,

"10 seeds here, 10 seeds there,
10 seeds in each handful, I plant them with care."
Johnny ended up planting 8 handfuls of seeds. He also planted 6 extra seeds.

How many seeds did he plant in all? _____

How many in each group?

What patterns do you see?

Name _____

Paul's Peanut Machine

Go Nuts Over Peanuts Week is the third week of March. To celebrate, Paul made a peanut machine.

When he put 2 peanuts in the machine, 12 came out.

When he put 5 peanuts in the machine, 15 came out.

When he put 6 peanuts in the machine, 16 came out.

What would happen if he puts in 7, 8, or 10 peanuts? _____

What is the machine doing? _____

Name _____

Mark's Baby Sister

Mark's baby sister Krista is 1 year old. Mark is 8 years old. Write the answers on the lines below.

When Krista is 1, Mark is 8.   When Krista is 2, Mark is _____.

When Krista is 3, Mark is _____.   When Krista is 4, Mark is _____

When Krista is 5, Mark is _____.   When Krista is 6, Mark is _____

When Krista is 7, Mark is _____.   When Krista is 8, Mark is _____

Circle the one where Mark's age is double his sister's age.

Name _____

Amusement Park Math

The amusement park opened on the first day of spring. 12 people were in line for the "Over the Falls" ride. 4 people fit in each boat. All the people got into their boats.

How many boats were filled? _____

Explain how you figured out the answer.

Name _____

Peter Piper's Pickled Peppers

In the fall, Peter Piper stored 26 jars of pickled peppers.
During the winter, he ate 7 jars of pickled peppers. Now it is spring.

How many jars does Peter have left? _____.

Write an equation to show your answer.

_____

Name _____

Would You Rather Have . . . ?

When Carrie put away her winter clothes, she found 5 dimes in her coat pocket. Her brother said he would trade her his 46 pennies for her 5 dimes.   Should she trade?

Circle Yes or No   **YES**   **NO**

Explain your answer. _____

_____

Classroom Garage Sale

Tolu's class did some spring cleaning. Then they had a garage sale.
They sorted the things they were selling. Sort these objects into like
groups. Draw the items of each group on one of the tables below.

_____   _____   _____

Below each table, write a label for the group.

Patterns for the Mail Carrier

Meimei the mail carrier is delivering letters. Give her some help.
Fill in the missing addresses on the houses below.

Extra

What pattern do you see in the house numbers? _____

_____

_____

77

Name _____

Bird Feeder Geometry

It's spring! The birds are coming back. Kwaku and his mother made two bird feeders. What shapes can you find on their feeders? Write your ideas on the lines.

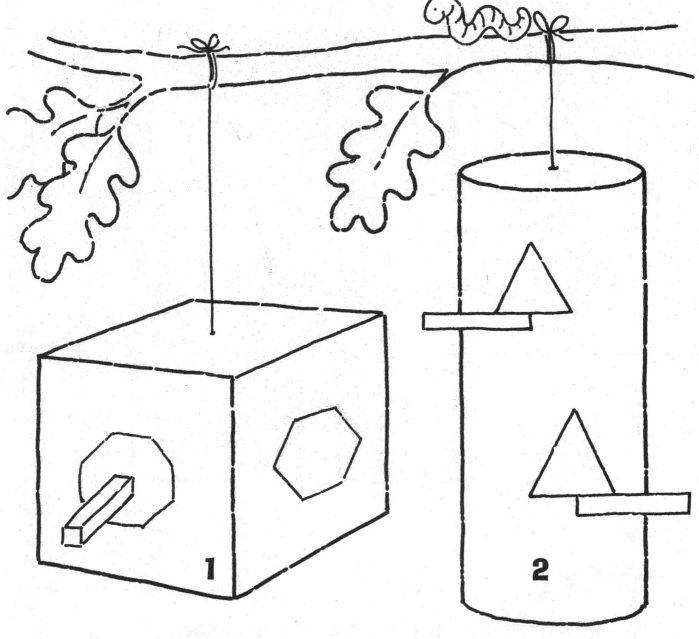

_____   _____

_____   _____

_____   _____

April

Name _____

Money, Addition

April Fool's?

On April Fool's Day, Jeff said to his mom, "I'd rather have 2 dimes and 13 pennies than 3 dimes and 2 pennies." Do you think this was an April Fool's Day joke?

Circle Yes or No.   **YES**   **NO**

Explain your answer: _____

_____

Name _____

Division

Party Balloons

At the end of the April Fool's Party, Li divided the balloons. He had 15 balloons for 3 children. "The balloons don't divide evenly!" said Li. Is he right?

Circle Yes or No.   **YES**   **NO**

Explain your answer: _____

How many balloons does each child get? _____

Name _____

Ricky Recycles

Every Friday, Ricky takes the recycling bin to the curb.

Look at a calendar. How many times will Ricky take out the recycling bin in April? _____

How many times in May? _____ How many times in June? _____

How many times altogether in April, May, and June? _____

Write an equation to show your last answer. _____

Name _____

Baseball Shapes

Baseball season starts in April. A baseball field is made up of many shapes.
Look at this baseball field. What shapes do you see?

_____   _____

_____   _____

Draw the baseball field on a bigger sheet of paper. Label the shapes.

Name _____

Donuts in a Bag

Davey bought some donuts for his class. 6 donuts were in the bag.
4 were sugar donuts. 2 were glazed donuts.

If you reached in the bag without looking,
what kind of donut would you probably get? _____

Explain your answer. _____

Extra: Try this activity with colored tiles.

Name _____

Benny's One-Man Band

Benny Bunny is a one-man band. He needs to take a boat to the Spring Parade. The boat holds 27 pounds.

6 lbs   5 lbs   2 lbs   4 lbs   8 lbs

How much does Benny and his instruments weigh? _____

Can the boat hold Benny and all his instruments? _____

Name _____

A Tricky Way to Tell Time

Jack doesn't use numbers to tell the time. Instead, he describes how the clock hands look. Try Jack's method. Tell what time it is:

1. The hands are shaped like the letter L. _____

2. The hands are shaped like a backwards L. _____

3. The hands are straight up and down. They are on top of each other. _____

4. The hands are straight up and down. They are not on top of each other. _____

Name _____

Barnyard Patterns

At the farm, it was time to shoe the horses. Jayson was counting the horses' hooves. Give him a hand.

How many total hooves for 2 horses? _____   How many total hooves for 3 horses? _____

How many total hooves for 4 horses? _____   How many total hooves for 5 horses? _____

How many total hooves for 6 horses? _____

Name _____

Animal Garden Addition

Solve this math problem.

Bunny planted 24 carrot seeds.
Raccoon planted 13 bean seeds.
When all the seedlings start to grow,
how many new plants will there be? _____

Write an equation to show your answer. _____

Name _____

The Ants Get Their Exercise

Anna Ant lived in a garden. For exercise, she jogged around blocks of wood. Measure all the sides of each block to the nearest inch. Write your measurement on each line.

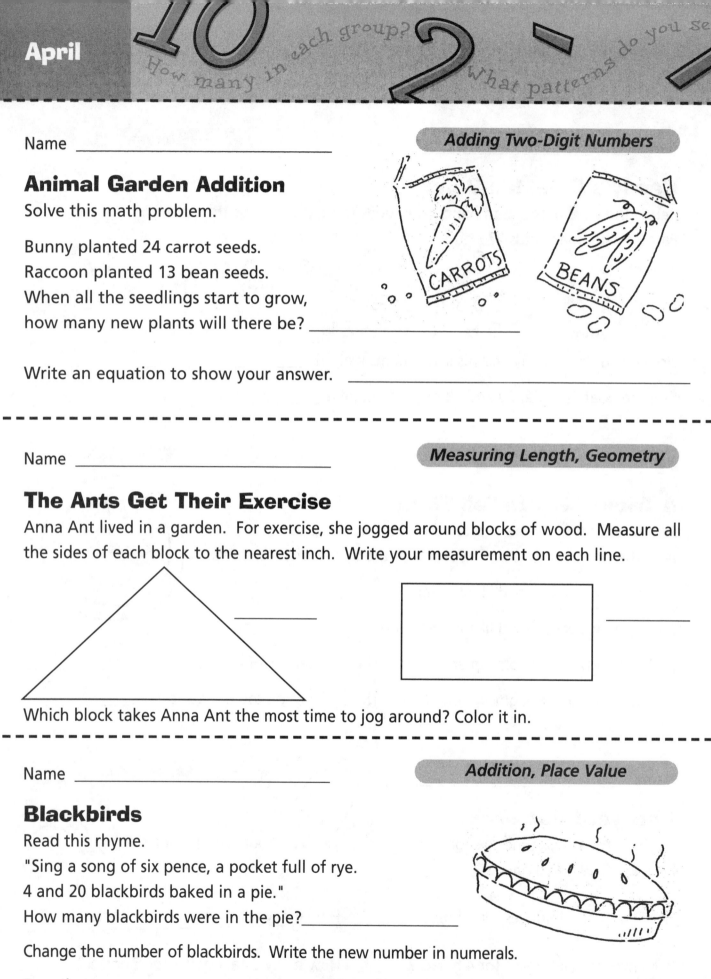

Which block takes Anna Ant the most time to jog around? Color it in.

Name _____

Blackbirds

Read this rhyme.

"Sing a song of six pence, a pocket full of rye.
4 and 20 blackbirds baked in a pie."
How many blackbirds were in the pie?_____

Change the number of blackbirds. Write the new number in numerals.

Equation: _____   Numeral: _____

Name _____

A Prickly Problem

Mrs. Porcupine was sorting shapes.
This is what she did:

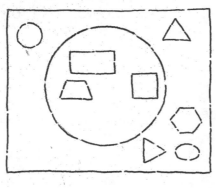

Where do these shapes go?

Draw the shapes in the correct place.

Name _____

The Biggest Number

It was time for the Math Olympics. The Ladybug Team had the numbers 2, 3, 4, and 5 on their backs. Their challenge was to make the largest sum they could using the numbers on their backs. Write the numbers in the boxes to make the largest sum.

Name _____

Planting Beans

Tom planted 23 jellybeans and 16 string beans.
How many "beans" did he plant in all?
Place the numbers in these boxes to add and find out.

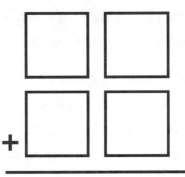

Extra: Which "beans" do you think really grew?
Write your answer on the back.

How many in each group?

What patterns do you see?

Name _____

Subtracting Two-Digit Numbers

Mr. McGregor's Garden

Peter Rabbit went into Mr. McGregor's garden to eat the carrots. He counted 30 carrots. He nibbled on 10 before he heard Mr. McGregor's footsteps.

How many carrots did he leave alone? _____

Explain how you figured out the answer. _____

_____

Name _____

Addition

Farm Animals Weigh In

Jody helped her mom weigh the baby animals on the farm.

The baby goat weighed 12 pounds.
The chick weighed 2 pounds.
The lamb weighed 7 pounds.
The piglet weighed 19 pounds.

_____   _____

_____

Then she put 2 animals on one side of a large balance scale and 1 animal on the other side. The scale balanced! Which animals did she put on each side? Write their names on the line.

Name _____

Place Value

Groups of Geese

In April, when the weather is warm, geese fly north. They fly in the shape of an upside down V. 37 geese are flying north. Each V has 10 geese.

How many groups of 10 are there? _____

How many geese are left over? _____

Name _____

Money, Addition

National Coin Week

The fourth week of April is National Coin Week. Joan and John found 3 dimes and 4 nickels.
How can they divide the money so each gets the same amount?

Joan could get _____ dime(s) and _____ nickel(s).

John could get _____ dime(s) and _____ nickel(s).

Name _____

Fractions, Division

Billy Goat's Raisins

The billy goat needed to cross the bridge. A troll stopped him.
"Give me your raisins," said the troll.
"I'll share them with you," said the billy goat. "I have 24 raisins.
You can have half. Tell me how many you should get."
While the troll was figuring out the problem, the billy goat
went right on by, keeping all his raisins.

What answer should the troll have come up with? _____
Hint: Use manipulatives to figure out the answer.

Name _____

Creature Categories

Nick's class took a field trip to the beach. When they looked in the tide pools, they saw a lot of animals. Group the animals they saw. Color the animals in each group the same color.

Write a word or phrase that explains how you grouped them.

Group #1 _____

Group #2 _____

Group #3 _____

Time to Get Up!

Twenty animals were hibernating near Sleepy Pond.
5 of them woke up. Color 5 animals below.

How many are still sleeping? _____

A week later, 7 more woke up.   Color 7 other animals.

How many are still sleeping? _____

Jack's Beanstalk

Jack's class was growing bean plants.   After 1 week,
Jack's was the tallest.

Measure Jack's plant below.   Record its height: _____

After 2 weeks, Jack's plant had doubled in height.

How tall was it now? _____

Draw a picture to show how tall the plant grew.
Measure your drawing to make sure it is the correct height.

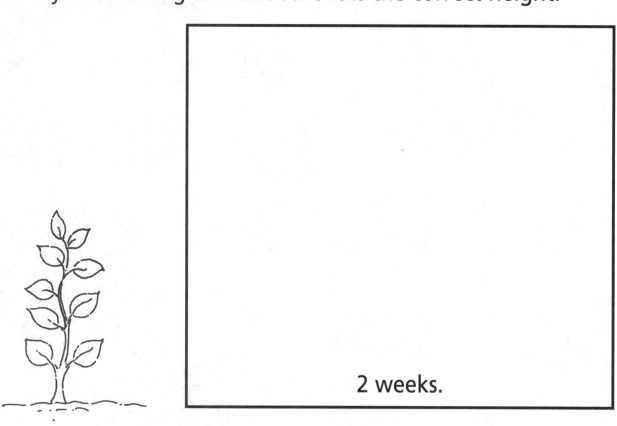

2 weeks.

After 3 weeks, Jack's plant was still growing!

How tall would it be now? _____

Explain your answer. _____

May

Name _____

Ice-Cream Favorites

Take a class survey. First, copy the Venn diagram below on a sheet of paper. Make it as big as possible. Then ask your classmates which they like more—chocolate ice cream or strawberry ice cream. Write their names in the correct circle. If they like both flavors equally, write their names in the center circle. If they don't like either one, write their names outside the circle.

How many like chocolate?_____

How many like strawberry?_____

How many like both? _____

Name _____

Shape Riddles

Solve these shape riddles. Try to picture the shapes in your mind.

I have 6 sides, and all of them are square.
I'm number cubes, I'm blocks. I'm everywhere.

What solid shape am I? _____

I'm orange at a construction site, and ice cream sits on top of me.
You sometimes run around me when you're playing in P. E.

What solid shape am I? _____

How many in each group? What patterns do you see?

Name _____

Getting Ready

It took Dina's grandmother 1 1/2 hours to braid Dina's hair.   She started at 11:00 in the morning.

At what time did she finish? _____

The party was at 1:00.
Did Dina's grandmother finish braiding Dina's hair in time for her to go to the party?

Circle Yes or No.   **YES**   **NO**

Extra: How much extra time did they have? _____

Name _____

Snoozing in May

May is "Better Sleep Month." Using a calculator, Kezia taught Jamal how to figure out how many hours a week he sleeps. This is what she did. She pushed **8+** on the calculator. Then she pushed the + key 6 more times. Try it! Write the number on the calculator each time you push the keys.

Day 1: + _____   Day 2: + _____

Day 3: + _____   Day 4: + _____

Day 5: + _____   Day 6: + _____

Day 7: + _____

Name _____

Cluck, Neigh, Moo

Figure out the pattern of the barnyard symphony below. Fill in the missing sounds.

Cluck, neigh, meow,   Oink, _____, _____,

Cluck, neigh, moo.   Oink, _____, _____,

Woof, neigh, meow,   Cock-a-doodle, doodle, doo.

Woof, _____, _____.

Name _____

Birthdays in May

Sam and Danielle both have birthdays in May. Sam's birthday is 3 weeks away.
Danielle's birthday is 18 days away.

Whose birthday comes first? _____

Explain your answer. _____

_____

Name _____

Spider Survey

In May many spiders make their webs. Do you like spiders? Do your classmates?
Take a class survey.   Draw a tally mark next to each.

Do Like Spiders _____   **Do Not Like Spiders** _____

How many of your classmates like spiders? _____

How many classmates do not like them? _____

Write the numbers in a greater than/less than equation: _____ > _____

Name _____

Mother's Day Decisions

Sera went to the store with 30¢ to buy a gift for Mother's Day.
She bought 2 things. Circle 2 gifts she could buy with 30¢.

10¢   12¢

How much money did Sera spend? _____

How much did she have left? _____

15¢   5¢

91

How many in each group? What patterns do you see?

Name _____

Spring Shelter

The wildlife shelter received two new animals. The new raccoon has 5 toes on each foot.
The new parrot has 4 toes on each foot.

Total number of raccoon toes: _____

Total number of parrot toes: _____

The raccoon has _____ more toes than the parrot.

Name _____

Critical Thinking

Heads and Feet

Solve this math riddle.

Chickens are clucking in the hen house. Horses are neighing in the barn.
There are 12 legs and 4 heads altogether, making a racket on Grandma's farm.

How many horses are on the farm? _____

How many chickens are on the farm? _____

Hint: Draw a picture on the back to find the answer.

Name _____

Adding Two-Digit Numbers

International Pickle Week

The third week of May is International Pickle Week.
Jeffrey's class had a pickle picnic. They had 35 dill pickles and 32 sweet pickles.

How many pickles in total were at the pickle picnic? _____
On the back, show how you figured out the answer.

Name _____

"Bee" a Mathematician

Kathy watches a beehive from her window.
She notices that no bee works in a cell that touches
another cell. Draw bees in the cells to show
what Kathy sees. One bee is drawn in for you.

How many bees are working in this beehive?

_____

Name _____

Parade Hats

For the May Day parade, 27 children and 7 adults were playing in the marching band.
The band ordered 35 fancy hats with feathers.

Did everyone get a hat?

Circle Yes or No.   **YES**   **NO**

Write an equation to explain your answer _____

Name _____

Cricket Jumps

A cricket jumped along a number line. He took equal jumps to the number 12.
He could do this in 4 ways.
Circle the numbers he jumped on. (Hint: He didn't start on 1.)

Jump #1: 1 2 3 4 5 6 7 8 9 10 11 12   Jump #3: 1 2 3 4 5 6 7 8 9 10 11 12

Jump #2: 1 2 3 4 5 6 7 8 9 10 11 12   Jump #4: 1 2 3 4 5 6 7 8 9 10 11 12

Zoo Weigh-In

Zoey's class went to the zoo. They wrote down how much the animals weighed. Cut out the animals below. Arrange them in weight order—from lightest to heaviest.

329 lbs

358 lbs.

224 lbs.

532 lbs.

Name _____

Chester's Cakes and Pies

Fill in the blanks. Chester Chipmunk was cutting cakes and pies.
Bobby Bear said, "Some aren't cut in half.

When you cut something in half, there are _____

pieces and both of the pieces are the same _____."

Here is how Chester cut the cakes and pies.
Circle the desserts that are cut in half correctly.

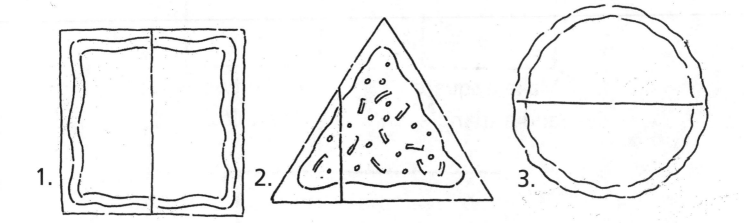

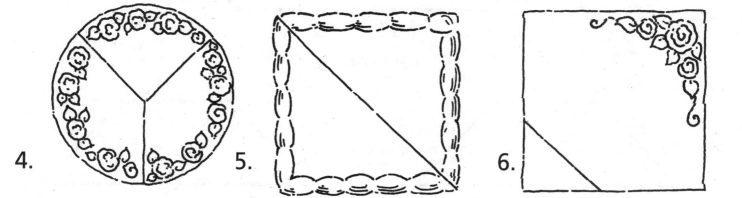

Name _____

Shape Tricks

Danny's class was learning about shapes. He noticed that you could draw a line across one shape to make two shapes. Draw a line through each shape below to make two new shapes. (Hint: Pattern blocks may help you.)

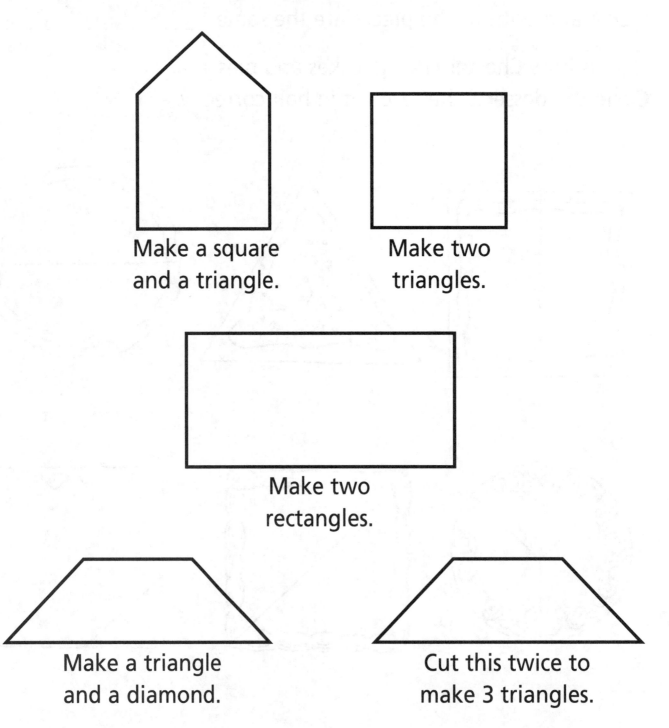

Make a square and a triangle.

Make two triangles.

Make two rectangles.

Make a triangle and a diamond.

Cut this twice to make 3 triangles.

Candy Boxes

Steve works in a candy store. He puts candy into boxes. Each box has 10 spaces. Steve has 32 candies. Try to draw 32 candies in the boxes below. Write the number of candies in each box on the line. Write the number of any leftover candy at the bottom of the page.

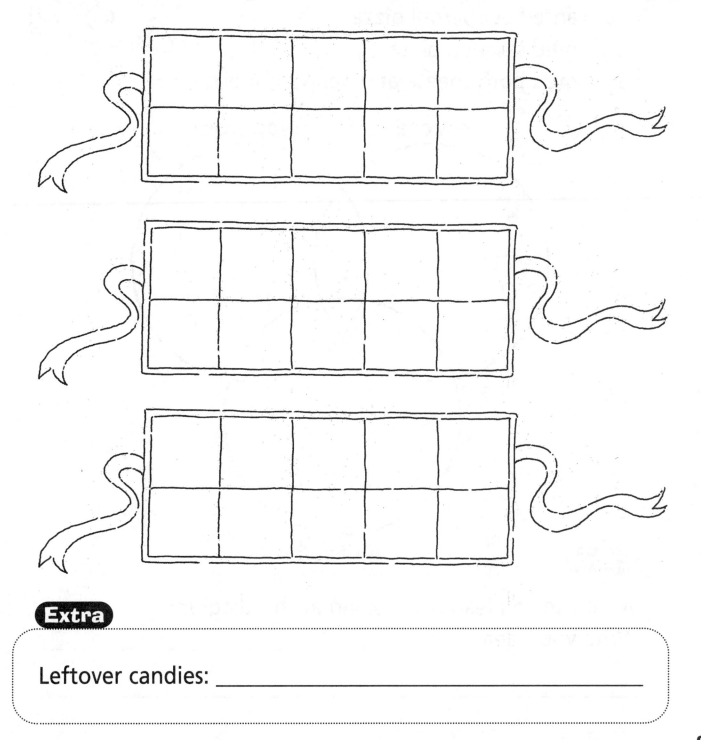

Extra

Leftover candies: _____

Pizza Party

Garth's class is having a pizza party. They made a diagram to show which pizzas they would like. Draw an X in each circle to show how many classmates wanted each kind of pizza.

- 5 wanted cheese pizza.
- 10 wanted pepperoni pizza.
- 3 wanted sausage pizza.
- 2 wanted both cheese and pepperoni pizza.

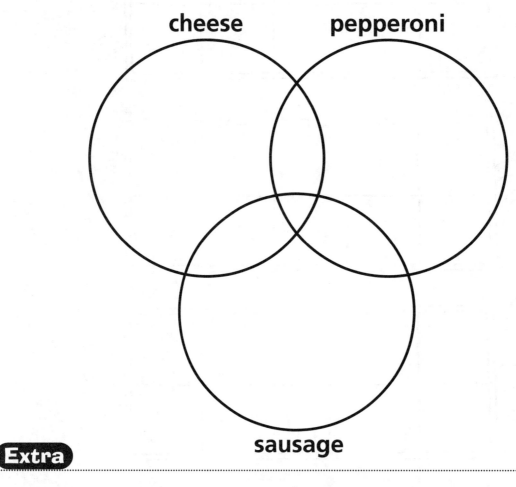

cheese   pepperoni

sausage

Extra

What can you learn by looking at this diagram?

Write your ideas: _____

_____

June

Name _____

Recognizing Patterns, Addition

Picnic Patterns

Figure out the pattern below by filling in the correct numbers.

5 flies, 8 chickadees

11 gnats, _____ fleas

_____ ants, and _____ bees

Are all at the picnic with you and me.

What pattern do the numbers have? _____

Name _____

Graphing, Comparing

Favorite Ball Games

Which ball games do your classmates like to play?
Record their answers on a bar graph, like the one below

Soccer								
Baseball								

Look at your graph. Complete this sentence with information you learn from the graph.

More children like_____ than_____ .

99

How many in each group? What patterns do you see?

Name _____

Father's Day

Father's Day is in June. Look at the letters of the word FATHER. Figure out which letters have symmetry. (You should be able to fold them in half and get two matching parts.) Remember, you can fold them in half in different directions. For example:

 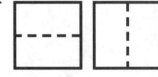

Write the letters that are symmetrical here: _____
Draw a line through each letter to show the symmetry.

Name _____

She Sells Seashells

Solve this math tongue-twister riddle.

She sells seashells by the seashore.

If each seashell sells for 3¢,
how much do 6 seashells cost? _____

Name _____

Baseball Scores

Jesse's team was playing baseball with Harry's team. Look at the scoreboard below. Add the numbers.

| Jesse | 1 | 4 | 0 | 2 | 0 | 1 | 0 | 0 | 2 | Total _____ |
| Harry | 2 | 2 | 0 | 3 | 1 | 2 | 0 | 0 | 1 | Total _____ |

Who won? Show the winner in a greater than/less than equation _____ > _____

Winner _____

Name _____

Flag Day Patterns

Look at the flag of the United States.
Color in the flag here so it looks like the
flag in your classroom.

What patterns do you see on the flag? On the
back of this paper, or on another sheet, list all
the patterns. Then describe the patterns, or
draw them. Hint: How many stars in each row?

Name _____

Spinners for the School Fair

Joey was making spinners for a game booth at
the school fair. Each spinner had a red section
and a white section. Look at the spinners below.
Which spinners are fair?
(Hint: A fair spinner has the same chance of landing on
a red section as a white section.) Circle the fair spinners.

Extra: On the back, explain why one spinner is not fair.

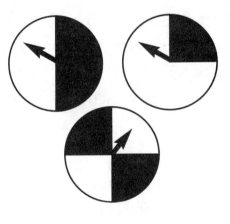

Name _____

Quilt Squares

Lenny's class is making a class quilt for the
end of the year. Each child can use two colors.
On the back, or on another sheet of paper,
draw quilt squares with two colors. Each color
must cover 1/2 of the square.

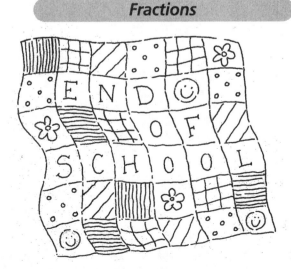

How many in each group?   What patterns do you see?

Name _____

365 Days to Go

Shauna's birthday was today. Her next birthday will be in 365 days. That's one whole year.

How many hundreds is that? _____

How many tens is that? _____

How many ones is that? _____

Extra: A leap year has 366 days. How many hundreds, tens, and ones are in a leap year?

Name _____

Pizza Party Puzzler

The porcupines had a pizza party on the last day of school. Peter Porcupine was very hungry. Should he have 1/4 of a pizza or 1/3 of a pizza?

_____

Look at these pizzas. Circle the correct one to show which fraction is more.

All Sorts of Animals

Milo's class learned about all sorts of animals. Look at the animals below. Cut them out. Sort them into groups that show how some animals are alike. Then share your groups with a friend. Did you sort them in the same way?

Favorite Class Subject

Which subjects do you and your classmates like the most?
Ask them to find out. Read each subject in the bar graph on
this page. Color in the square's to show each vote.

Math

Science

Reading

Geography

Social Studies

Art

P. E.

Music

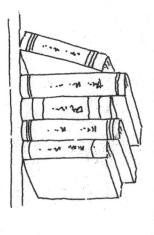

Answer Key

September

The Name Game, p. 7
Answers will vary but should reflect
the correct number of letters in each name.

Name Sort, p. 7
Answers will vary, but should accurately reflect the number of students in class. Other sorting ideas include: names that start with vowels, names that start with consonants; names with 1 syllable, 2 syllables, and so on; names with same beginning letters, names with same ending letters.

Off to School, p. 8
Answers will vary.

One Friend a day, p. 8
7, 7 Extra: 14

More Than 10, Less Than 10, p. 8
Answers will vary, depending on the group you set up.

Hide-and-Seek Countdown, p. 9
8 . . . 5, 4 . . . 2 Extra: 19 . . . 16 . . . 13, 12

Apple Colors, p. 9
Answers will vary.

Adding in Code, p. 9
EE, OU, E . . . E (THREE, FOUR, SEVEN)

Pencil Puzzler, p. 10
6 - 4 = 2, 2 + 2 = 4
Katie now has 4 pencils.

One Bee in Our Classroom, p. 10
7, 9

Apple Problems, p. 10
4, 4, Extra: 5, 5; 6, 6; 7, 7; 8, 8; 9, 9

Shapes All Around, p. 11
Answers will vary, but should reflect actual classroom objects and correct shape names.

Red, Black, Snap, Clap, p. 11
Black, black, red; ABBABBABBA
Extra: snap, clap, clap, snap, clap, clap snap

The Last Leaves, p. 11
The maple tree has 8 leaves. 5 + 3 = 8

Falling Leaves, p. 12
7 Extra: Answers will vary.

Classroom Zoo, p. 12
Groups: mice (3), turtles (3), fish (3)

Who Needs Glasses?, p. 12
14; 2, 4, 6, 8, 10, 12, 14

Frog School, p. 13
Extra: 2

Big Foot, p. 14
Estimates will vary. Actual length is 5".

Mary Had a Little Puppy, p. 15
followed, above, under, in, up

Fall Leaf Patterns, p. 16
Leaf patterns will vary.

October

Coin Detective, p. 17
The dime is smaller than the nickel, but it's worth more.

Finger-Adding Game, p. 17
Answers will vary.

Finding Favorite Colors, p. 18
Answers will vary, but should reflect the rows of color tiles students set up.

Falling Pumpkins, p. 18
7

Waiting in Line, p. 18
6, 10

One and Only One, p. 19
5 - 4 = 1   3 - 2 = 1   4 - 3 = 1   2 - 1 = 1

Shape Hunters, p. 19
1. cylinder   2. sphere   3. cone   4. cube   5. rectangular or cube

Poodles and Beagles, p. 19
2 poodles + 6 beagles = 8 dogs in all   3 poodles + 5 beagles = 8 dogs in all
4 poodles + 4 beagles = 8 dogs in all   5 poodles + 3 beagles = 8 dogs in all
6 poodles + 2 beagles = 8 dogs in all   7 poodles + 1 beagles = 8 dogs in all

Big Bad Wolf Math, p. 20
1. handspan   2. giant step   3. giant step   4. handspan

National Cookie Month, p. 20
3 Extra: 4

Disappearing Counting Cubes, p. 20
Answers will vary.

Nan's Number Cubes, p. 21

Jack-o'-Lantern Designer, p. 21
Answers will vary.

Three Halloween Kittens, p. 21
4 + 1 + 5 = 10   4 + 2 + 4 = 10   4 + 5 + 1 = 10   4 + 4 + 2 = 10   4 + 3 + 3 = 10

Trick or Treat?, p. 22
yes; 3 + 2 = 5; 2 + 3 = 5

Comparing Costumes, p. 22
3; 11 - 8 = 3

What's Your Costume?, p. 22
Answers will vary. Graph should be set up as a bar graph.
Answers should reflect information from the graph.

A Friendly Scarecrow, p. 23
4, 2 + 2 = 4
Extra: 6, 8, The numbers are double.

Sign Shape, p. 24
Yield sign: triangle, 3   Caution sign: diamond, 4
Speed-limit sign: rectangle, 4   Stop sign: octagon, 8

Ladybug Dots, p. 25
4 + 4 = 8   5 + 5 = 10   6 + 6 = 12   7 + 7 = 14   8 + 8 = 16
Extra: 6, 8, 10, 12, 14, 16   Pattern: Count by 2s, even numbers, doubling

Sorting Treats, p. 26
Great than: 10: 12 chocolate bars, 11 pennies, 15 pieces of gum, 13 candied apples.
Less than: 10: 7 boxes of raisins, 8 lollipops, 4 oranges, 1 cookie

November

Piggy Bank Puzzle, p. 27
dimes; nickels

Favorite Pet Tally, p. 27
Answers will vary. The favorite pet is the animal with the most tallies.

Playing in the Snow, p. 28
6 + 6 + 12,   6 + 7 = 13

ABC Sort, p. 28
Possible categories: vowels and consonants; letter will all curved lines, all straight lines, and both curved and straight lines; letters with and without symmetry; the number of strokes it takes to make each letter.

How Many Birthdays?, p. 28
4, 11 - 7 = 4 Extra: 15

Game and Puzzle Week, p. 29
2 + 7 = 9   9 - 2 = 7   7 + 2 = 9   9 - 7 = 2

Birthday Riddle, p. 29
9

Sledding Time, p. 29
Example: How many children in all?   5 + 3 = 8
How many more girls than boys?   5 - 3 = 2

Wildlife Shelter, p. 30
45 > 39, 45 > 28   28 < 39, 28 < 45   39 > 28, 39 < 45

Mystery Drawing, p. 30
Students should draw a turkey.

Gobbler Riddle, p. 30
1 + 9 = 10   2 + 8 = 10   3 + 7 = 10   4 + 6 = 10
5 + 5 = 10   6 + 4 + 10   7 + 3 = 10
8 + 2 = 10   9 + 1 = 10

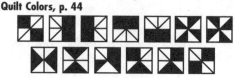
Thanksgiving Puzzler, p. 31
11-3=8
Possible answer: The more you take away from 11, the smaller the answer is.

Mystery Holiday, p. 31
11th month: November   Date: Answers will vary.   Holiday: Thanksgiving

Mashed, Baked, or Fried?, p. 31
Answers will vary.

Scavenger Hunt, p. 32
Answers will vary.

Collecting Food, p. 33
The answer could be a graph with 3 cans of chili, 3 cans of veggies, and 4 cans of soup.

Money Matters, p. 34
Alex's coins: 5¢ + 25¢ + 10¢ = 60 ¢
Billy's coins: 10¢ + 10¢ + 10¢ + 10¢ + 10¢ + 5¢ + 5¢ + 1¢ + 1¢ + 1¢ = 63¢
63¢ > 60¢   Billy has more money.

Penguin Family on Parade, p. 35
3 1/2 inches, 2 inches, 1 1/2 inches, 3 inches.   Patty, Peter, Petunia, Paul.

Thanksgiving Play, p. 36
2; Pilgrims, 4; Native Americans, Extra: 6,2

December

One and Off the Bus, p. 37
5; 4 - 2 = 2; 2 + 3 = 5

Magic Tricks, p. 37
Trick 1: 6 - 6 = 0   Trick 2: 0 + 5 = 5

Beehive Hexagons, p. 38

Basketball Time, p. 38
1 minute, 5 minutes, 2 hours

Barn Owl's Mistake, p. 38
Wrong answers: 4 + 5 = 7, 6 + 7 = 11   Correct answers: 4 + 5 = 9, 6 + 7 = 13
Barn owl is doubling and subtracting 1, instead of doubling and adding 1.

Cold Fingers and Toes, p. 39
Children could skip count by fives or tens.
Multiplication: 4 x 20 = 80; or 5 x 16 = 80; or 4 x 10 (fingers) = 40 fingers;
4 x 10 toes = 40 toes; 40 + 40 = 80

Two by Two, p. 39
Answers will vary. If the class has an even number of students, each student will have a partner. If the class has an odd number of students, one student will not have a partner.

The Goldfish Gift, p. 39
Possible answers: 1 quarter; 25 pennies; 2 dimes + 1 nickel; 2 dimes + 5 pennies;
1 dime + 3 nickels; 1 dime + 2 nickels + 5 pennies; 1 dime + 1 nickel + 10 pennies;
5 nickels, 15 pennies + 1 dime; 15 pennies + 2 nickels; 20 pennies + 1 nickel

Exactly in the Middle, p. 40
65

Pie Slices, p. 40
1; 2 Extra: 3

A Nickel a Month, p. 40
60¢; 5 x 12 = 60   5, 10, 15, 20, 25, 30, 35, 40, 45, 50, 55, 60

Thumb Prints and Hand Spans, p. 41
hand span; answers will vary; answers will vary (Note: The total number of hand spans should be less than the total number of thumb prints.)

A Wingful of Books, p. 41
You need to know the total number of books Owl took out.
Answers will vary, but should include the number 7: [student's number] - 7 = _____

Holiday Piggy Bank, p. 41
4 pennies; 5 pennies; 15

Family Time at Holiday Time, p. 42
Answers will vary.

Holiday Cookies, p. 42
1 carrot + 9 sugar = 10 cookies   2 carrot + 8 sugar = 10 cookies
3 carrot + 7 sugar = 10 cookies   4 carrot + 6 sugar = 10 cookies
5 carrot + 5 sugar = 10 cookies   6 carrot + 4 sugar = 10 cookies
7 carrot + 3 sugar = 10 cookies   8 carrot + 2 sugar = 10 cookies
9 carrot + 1 sugar = 10 cookies

Snowflakes on Mittens, p. 43
Estimates will vary. 2, 4, 6, 8, 10, 12, 14, 16, 18, 20, 5, 10, 15, 20
Extra: no; Snowflakes would melt before you could count them.

Quilt Colors, p. 44
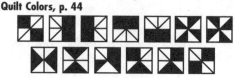

Cabin in the Snow, p. 45
6, 5, 4 Extra: hexagon—snowflake, pentagon—cabin, rectangle—doorway, circle—pancake

December Weather, p. 46
Sunny days: 12   Cloudy days: 8   Rainy days: 5   Snowy days: 6

January

Muffins by the Dozen, p. 47
7; 12 - 5 = 7

Rolling and Stacking, p. 47
sphere, cylinder, cube, cylinder

Penguin School, p. 48
5; Without weekends, a week has only 5 days.
Extra: 10

Guess My Number, p. 48
33, 34, 35, 36; no
Possible hints: It is an odd number. Both numerals are the same. You can get there if you skip count by 3's. It's less than 34.

Hibernation Breaks, p. 48
a cube; 4 (A cylinder has 2 flat sides. A cube has 6.)

Danny Duck's Dinner, p. 49
snail, ant.

Winter Boots and Socks, p. 49
Students might say that the boots weigh more because they are bigger and because they are wet.

Riddle Time, p. 49
6 (2, 4, 6, 8, 10; 3, 6, 9)

MLK, Jr.'s Birthday, p. 50
January 15

All Lined Up, p. 50
Bo, Mindy, Jane, Tim

Cathy's Cast, p. 50
January 28

Cool Calculations, p. 51
4 + 4 + 4 + 4 = 16; 4 + 4 + 3 = 11

Bear Family Quilts, p. 51

Temperature Matcheroo, p. 51
90°—summer   70°—spring   50°—fall   30°—winter

Favorite Number Graph, p. 52
Answers will vary.

Squirrel Math, p. 52
Pile #1: 10 Pile #2: 10 Pile #3: 10 Pile #4: 6
10 + 10 + 10 + 6 = 36

Pie Fight, p. 52
15; 26—11 = 15

National Popcorn Day, p. 53
Estimates will vary. Answers will vary. Greater than/less than equations will vary.

Coin Puzzler, p. 53
1 dime, 1 nickel, 1 penny
Extra: 2 dimes, 1 nickel, 1 penny

Scarf Patterns, p. 54
Pattern #1: triangle, heart, triangle, heart, triangle, heart
Pattern #2: little star, big star, little star, big star, little star, big star
Pattern #3: sun, cloud, cloud, sun, sun, cloud

What to Wear?, p. 55
Total amount of outfits = 6
Answers to second question will vary.

Dalmatian Spots, p. 56
Answers (estimates) will vary.   Total amount: 50
Skip count by 5's: 5, 10, 15, 20, 25, 30, 35, 40, 45, 50

February

Chinese New York, p. 57
3 quarters; 3 quarters is 75¢, which is more than 7 dimes, which is only 70¢.

Ground Hog Day, p. 57
12:00

Black History Month, p. 58
no; 39 + 3 = 42, not 43

Pennies and Paper Clips, p. 58
Answers will vary. When experimenting, students should discover that the pennies will be heavier, but the paper clips will be longer.

100th Day of School, p. 58
Estimates will vary. 10, 20, 30, 40, 50, 60, 70, 80, 90, 100; 10

Thirsty, Anyone?, p. 59
Answers will vary.

Bear Riddles, p. 59
polar bear; grizzly bear

President Pictures, p. 59
13 dollars; 5 dollars + 5 dollars = 10 dollars
1 dollar + 1 dollar + 1 dollar = 3 dollars
10 dollars + 3 dollars = 13 dollars

Who Is Older?, p. 60
Ashley; January comes before February, so Ashley is about one month older than Josh.

Slopping Winter Boots, p. 60
6 Extra: 8

Odd + Odd, p. 60
1 + 7 = 8; 3 + 5 = 8
Two odd numbers always add up to an even number. One even number and one odd number always add up to an odd number.

So Many Stamps!, p. 61
2 rows of 6 stamps
3 rows of 4 stamps
4 rows of 3 stamps
6 rows of 2 stamps

Valentine Count, p. 61
18; 6 + 6 + 6 = 18, or 6 x 3 = 18

Special Birthday, p. 61
2; 20; 20; 2000; They all have 2s, or 2s and 0s.
Extra: Turning 9 on September 9, 1999 (9/9/99)

Measuring His Shadow, pp. 62–63
10; 5; They were both right.

Snow-Print Detective, p. 64
stringed box = square
plant pot = triangle
drum = circle
book = rectangle

Valentine Symmetry, p. 65
symmetrical: heart, triangle, even V, hexagon
symmetrical twice: hexagon

Valentine Stickeroo, p. 66

O	O	X	X		X	X	O	O		X	O	X	O
O	X	O	X		X	O	O	X		O	X	X	O

Picking Out Patterns, p. 67
1. 32, 42, 52, 62, 72, 82, 92   2. 70, 60, 50, 40, 30, 20, 10
3. 67, 57, 47, 37, 27, 17, 7   4. 44, 55, 66, 77, 88, 99

Presidents' Day Problem, p. 68
1. the 1st   2. the 16th   3. James Buchanan   4. Andrew Johnson   5. 14

March

Colorful Kites, p. 69
Students' pictures should look like this:

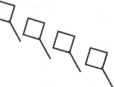

What's for Breakfast?, p. 69
Answers will vary.

The Three Bears' Orange Juice, p. 70
Possible estimates: 6 cups, 4 cups. Explanation: Baby Bear's thermos is about half the size of Papa Bear's thermos, or 4 cups. Mama Bear's thermos is about in between in size, or 6 cups.

Money Riddle, p. 70
15¢; 10 + 5 = 15
17¢; 15 + 2 = 17

The Shrinking Teddy Bear, p. 70
Thursday: 14 inches   Friday: 12 inches   Saturday: 10 inches
The bear could be shrinking because it has a hole and is losing stuffing.

Finding Gold, p. 71
12; 7 + 8 = 15; 15 - 3 = 12

Leprechaun Gold, p. 71
5; 6 or more; [student's answer] > 5

Leprechaun Steps, p. 71
Estimates will vary. Number of steps will vary.

Who Won?, p. 72
64; 46; 64 > 46; Jane's team won.

Dog Calculations, p. 72
10, 15, 20, 25

Lost-and-Found Mystery, p. 72
22; 26 - 4 = 22
Extra: Possible answer: Children wear jackets and sweatshirts in the wnter.

Kite Store, p. 73
50; 10 x 5 = 50 or 10+10+10+10+10=50

The Year of the Dragon, p. 73
22; 10 + 12 = 22

Johnny Appleseed Math, p. 73
86

Paul's Peanut Machine, p. 74
17, 18, 20; The machine is adding 10 more peanuts to the original amount put in the machine.

Mark's Baby Sister, p. 74
When Krista is 1, Mark is 8.   When Krista is 2, Mark is 9.
When Krista is 3, Mark is 10.   When Krista is 4, Mark is 11.
When Krista is 5, Mark is 12.   When Krista is 6, Mark is 13.
When Krista is 7, Mark is 14.   When Krista is 8, Mark is 15.
Double: When Krista is 7, Mark is 14.

Amusement Park Math, p. 74
3; 12 ÷ 4 = 3

Peter Piper's Pickled Peppers, p. 75
19; 26 - 7 = 19

Would You Rather Have . . .?, p. 75
no; 5 dimes = 50¢, which is more money than 46¢

Classroom Garage Sale, p. 76
Possible groups: Balls: soccer ball, basketball, rubber ball
Winter clothes: scarf, hat, boots   Art supplies: paint, paint brush, crayon

Patterns for the Mail Carrier, p. 77
Top side of the street: 50, 52, 54, 56   Bottom side of the street: 51, 53, 55
Extra: The even numbers are on one side of the street. The odd numbers are on the other side of the street.

Bird Feeder Geometry, p. 78
1. cube, octagon, hexagon, rectangle, square, rectangle solid
2. cyclinder, triangle, circle, rectangle

April

April Fools?, p. 79
no; 2 dimes + 13 pennies = 33¢;
This is more money than 3 dimes + 2 pennies, which is 32¢.

Party Balloons, p. 79
no; 15 ÷ 3 = 5 or three divides evenly into 15

Ricky Recycles, p. 80˜
Answers will vary, depending on current year's calendar. There will be 4–5 Fridays for each month. Number sentences will vary, but show all 3 numbers being added, for example, 4 + 5 + 4 = 13

Baseball Shapes, p. 80
bases = squares   home plate = pentagon
infield = diamond   pitcher's mound = circle and square

Donuts in a Bag, p. 80
sugar donut; There are more sugar donuts than glazed donuts.

Benny's One-Man Band, p. 81
25 pounds; yes

A Tricky Way to Tell Time, p. 81
1. 3:00, or 12:15   2. 9:00, or 11:45   3. 12:00   4. 6:00

Barnyard Patterns, p. 81
8 (2 x 4)   12 (3 x 4)   16 (4 x 4)   20 (5 x 4)   24 (6 x 4)

Animal Garden Addition, p. 82
37; 24 + 13 = 37

The Ants Get Their Exercise, p. 82
triangle: 7 inches
rectangle: 7 inches

Blackbirds, p. 82
24; students' new number sentences and numerals will vary. Make sure they
follow the same pattern as the rhyme, with the ones coming before the tens.

A Prickly Problem, p. 83
The rectangle and the parallelogram go inside the circle because all shapes here have
four sides. The triangle goes outside the circle because it does not have four sides.

The Biggest Number, p. 83
53 + 42 = 95

Planting Beans, p. 83
23 + 16 = 39
Extra: The string beans grew. Jelly beans are not real beans, but candy.

Mr. McGregor's Garden, p. 84
20; 30 - 10 = 20

Farm Animals Weigh In, p. 84
lamb and baby goat on one side; piglet on the other side

Groups of Geese, p. 84
3 groups of 10; 7 geese are left over

National Coin Week, p. 85
One child gets: 2 dimes + 1 nickel (25¢)   One child gets: 1 dime + 3 nickels (25¢)

Billy Goat's Raisins, p. 85
12

Creature Categories, p. 86
3 groups: fish, shells, animals with multiple legs/arms

Time to Get Up!, p. 87
15; 8

Jack's Beanstalk, p. 88
2 inches; 4 inches
Two possible answers:
6 inches, because it grew 2 inches each week; or
8 inches, because it doubled in height each week

May

Ice-Cream Favorites, p. 89
Answers will vary.

Shape Riddles, p. 89
cube; cone

Getting Ready, p. 90
12:30; yes; Extra: 1/2 hour or 30 minutes

Snoozing in May, p. 90
Day 1: 8   Day 2: 16   Day 3: 24   Day 4: 32   Day 5: 40   Day 6: 48   Day 7: 56

Cluck, Neigh, Moo, p. 90
Woof, neigh, moo; Oink, neigh, meow, neigh, moo

Birthdays in May, p. 91
Danielle; 3 weeks is 21 days, which is longer than 18 days.

Spider Survey, p. 91
Answers will vary.

Mother's Day Decisions, p. 91
Answers will vary.

Spring Shelter, p. 92
raccoon toes: 20   parrot toes: 8
12

Heads and Feet, p. 92
2 horses, 2 chickens

International Pickle Week, p. 92
67

"Bee" a Mathematician, p. 93
5,

Parade Hats, p. 93
yes; 27 + 7 = 34

Cricket Jumps, p. 93
Jump #1: 2, 4, 6, 8, 10, 12   Jump #2: 3, 6, 9, 12   Jump #3: 4, 8, 12   Jump #4: 6, 12

Zoo Weigh-In, p. 94
deer (224 pounds), seal (329 pounds), lion (358 pounds), bear (532 pounds)

Chester's Cakes and Pies, p. 95
2, size; Correct pies: 1, 3, 5

Shape Tricks, p. 96
1 (pentagon shape) 2 (square with diagonal) 3 (rectangle split) or (rectangle split vertically) — This line could move up or down. / This line could move left or right. 4 (trapezoid with triangles) 5 (trapezoid with triangles)

Candy Boxes, p. 97
10, 10, 10   Extra: 2

Pizza Party, p. 98
Extra: Answers will vary. Possible: Pepperoni is the most popular topping.
Cheese is the next favorite topping. Sausage is the least favorite topping.

June

Picnic Patterns, p. 99
14 fleas; 17 ants 20 bees
Pattern: Each number is the previous number plus 3.

Favorite Ball Games, p. 99
Answers will vary.

Father's Day, p. 100
A, T, H, E

She Sells Seashells, p. 100
18¢

Baseball Scores, p. 100
Jesse's total: 10   Harry's total: 11   11 > 10   winner: Harry

Flag Day Patterns, p. 101
red strip, white stripe, red stripe, white stripe;
horizontally, stars are in rows of 6, 5, 6, 5;
vertically, stars are in columns of 5, 4, 5, 4;
every other row of stars is indented

Spinners for the School Fair, p. 101
1. fair; the red and white sides are the same size.
2. not fair; the spinner would probably land on white because the white section
   is larger than the red section.
3. fair; both colors have two sections that are the same size.

Quilt Squares, p. 101
Possible answers:

365 Days to Go, p. 102
3 hundreds, 6 tens, 5 ones
Extra: 3 hundreds, 6 tens, 6 ones

Pizza Party Puzzler, p. 102
1/3, the pie with 3 pieces should be circled.

All Sorts of Animals, p. 103
Answers will vary. Possible ways to sort:
insects/fish/mammals; number of legs; live in air vs. water

Favorite Class Subject, p. 104
Answers will vary.